A SHETLAND KNITTER'S NOTEBOOK

A SHETLAND KNITTER'S NOTEBOOK

Knitting patterns and stories
selected and edited by
MARY SMITH

Photographs by
CHRIS BUNYAN

The Shetland Times Ltd
Lerwick
1991

ISBN: 0 900662 73 5

Front cover:
The Fair Isle Jumper, 1923
Stanley Cursiter (1887 - 1976)
City Art Centre, Edinburgh

Printed and published by
The Shetland Times Ltd.,
Lerwick, Shetland, Scotland

CONTENTS

THE SHETLAND ISLANDS

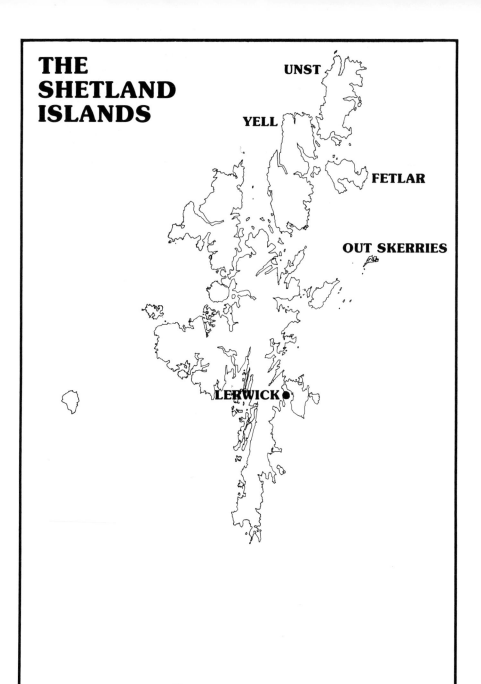

UNST

YELL

FETLAR

OUT SKERRIES

LERWICK●

 FAIR ISLE

INTRODUCTION

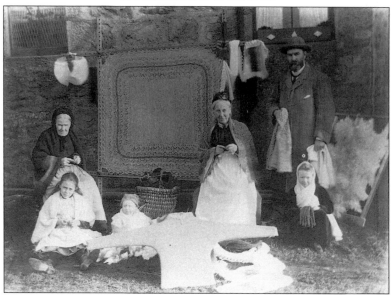

Old examples of knitting.

Ten years ago the 'knitting' shelf in most bookshops and libraries held a few ancient, grey, and predictable volumes on the twin-set and the matinée jacket. Since then a knitwear revolution has taken place, with top designers and chain stores vying to attract attention for their special collections. No longer is great aunt Aggie's gift of a hand-knit sweater hidden away in the bottom drawer.

This surge of interest has resulted in the publication of several specialist books on the knitwear of the Shetland Islands — the group of islands off the north-east coast of Scotland. In this cold, remote spot the craft of knitting has flourished for many years, and the skills of the Shetland knitters are known all over the world.

Traditional Shetland knitting takes two forms — the fine delicate lace work, nowadays most commonly associated with Unst, and Fair Isle which is two-colour knitting using intricate geometric and graphic patterns. Since the 1930s machine knitting, combined with hand knitting and finishing skills, has become a part of local industry. The versatile new table machines by Knitmaster, Jones and Singer, which knit Fair Isle and lace, have become more popular recently, but most work is still done on double bed machines such as Daplux, Dubied and Harrison, or the smaller Passap, which can produce tubular knitting and proper ribbing in keeping with the tradition of seamfree garments.

Most women can knit, and many do; although now more from habit than necessity. In the isles and remote parts of the Shetland Mainland

1

men also knitted, either to augment the family income or as an alternative to being unemployed. However, few of them enjoyed this type of work and today nearly all of those who knit do so on large industrial machines.

In Shetland many knitwear firms have come and gone over the years. These range from large factories producing plain garments for the mass market, to one-woman businesses dealing with private orders, but most medium-sized and small businesses, such as the one my husband and I ran for nine years, are operated as 'cottage industries'. Machine and hand knitting is done at home using the factory's wool and sometimes, if the knitter is prolific, the factory's machine. During the sixties in particular many husband and wife teams derived a good income from this arrangement; the man knitting on the machine and the woman grafting the jumper or putting in a Fair Isle yoke by hand. Recently many small businesses have adapted the old knitting skills to produce more fashionable garments, such as 'stripey' jumpers and Fair Isles in brighter, more exotic colour combinations. These experiments have generally proved successful and the products are sold throughout Britain and abroad.

Many women still prefer the independence of making up garments with their own wool, either producing the same work (such as gloves) on a regular basis, or creating something different, as the fancy takes them, according to the wool in their 'cloo bag'. This work is usually sold direct to the knitwear shops in Lerwick or sent to specialist stores in the south.

Over the past ten years the prosperity brought to Shetland by the Sullom Voe Oil Terminal has caused a decline in the knitwear industry. With this in mind, and realising that many of the traditional skills were in danger of becoming extinct, I decided to record some of the patterns, styles and memories of the older generation of knitters before they were lost. The patterns were noted and, where possible, examples of work were photographed. By looking at a photograph of a garment a skilled knitter can copy or improvise on the idea, but for those with simpler skills, or different talents, I have placed a pattern section at the back of the book.

I cannot claim to have produced a definitive work on Shetland knitwear but I have compiled a collection of patterns and information which appealed to me, and which I hope will interest and stimulate other knitters. I would like to extend my thanks for the kindness and hospitality shown to me on all my visits to the islands and on the Mainland, and to the numerous knitters whose advice and encouragement helped me produce this book. I hope it will be used for both pleasure and profit and that some readers will try out the old styles, perhaps modifying and personalising them, and so designing a unique range of woollens which will keep themselves, and their friends, and maybe even great aunt Aggie both warm and well-dressed for many years to come.

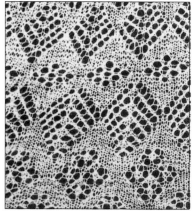

Section of fine lace shawl.

Allover on man.

Handknitter.

Knitter at machine.

Stripey jumper.

F.I. Base jumper.

3

OLD KNITTING CATALOGUE

Researching a book can be more exciting than writing it. The people, cups of tea and home-bakes, and the very special pieces of knitting I was shown helped in this task. Descriptions and photographs will never recreate the charm of seeing and handling a rare shawl or allover and hearing first-hand of its creation and the special details that make it totally unique.

Much of the old knitwear has left the isles, for the folk had to sell their work. The smart allovers seen today show the affluence of the islanders, who in former times sold their 'makkin' or more often exchanged it for food at the local merchants.

At the turn of the century the upper classes could well afford Shetland's products and this market was catered for by John White and Company's Shetland House situated at 30 Frederick Street, Edinburgh. Their mail order catalogue of 1908 was lent to me by an Unst lady. This old book fascinated me and I hope by describing its contents you too will be amazed at the wondrous array of garments worn by our forebears.

The cover shows a sketch of a Shetland 'wife' dressed in a striped 'cot' (skirt) with a 'hap' (shawl) over her head, busily knitting on her three 'wires' as she carries a 'kishie of peats' from the peatbank to the stack at her croft. Time was too precious to allow for idle hands.

Shawl.

Fine lace shawl.

The catalogue's fifty pages contain not only photographs and descriptions of the goods for sale but details of Shetland life and traditions. There are two colour plates and Willie's engraving, 1755, of the painting La Devideuse by Gerard Douw, which refers to the Shetland spinners who still used a wooden winder of the same shape for dividing wool into skeins. Even the chapter endings had small detailed engravings showing spinning wheels, kishies, and colly lamps made from conch shells.

Although the garments knitted today differ in style from those illustrated, the lace patterns are often the same — the puzzle, the spider's web, the shell, cat's paw and the print o' the wave. With improved building techniques and central heating we do not wear as many layers of clothing and certainly no one of my acquaintance has recently bought a cholera belt.

Shetland wool is described as soft, light and warm, and comes from the native sheep, a hardy breed, peculiar to the isles. They subsist on the sparse vegetation and seaweed. The fine wool is 'rooed' from the sheep, then cleaned, carded and spun. By 1908 most wool was spun on power looms at mills on the Scottish Mainland, although the very fine lace yarn was still spun by hand.

The natural colours — still the most popular — are a creamy white, dark brown known as Shetland black, shaela a greyish brown and, rarest of all, murat (moorit) a soft donkey brown. Shetland grey was a blend of brown and white.

Shetland spinner.

Winding hanks.

5

Shaded hap.

Lace headsquare.

Crepe Shawl.

Stole.

6

Shawls, so delicate and gossamer-like that they could be drawn through a wedding ring, were sold as evening wear, while haps, a warmer and thicker variation were used as baby shawls or for bedroom wear. Famous sanitoria used Shetland shawls as bedcovers because of their lightness and warmth. Knitters' styles, patterns and qualities varied and so did prices, with a one yard square shawl costing between 3s 6d and 7s 6d, and a two and a half yard square shawl costing from 35s to 50s. Black shawls, for fashion or mourning, cost an extra 2s. Thicker haps, often with a shaded, wavy shell border, cost from 28s to 38s for a two and a half yard square. Today similar shawls in Edinburgh cost upwards of £35. A lace headsquare 20" by 36", cost 3s 6d to 10s and the finest lace shawls, weighing a mere two ounces were priced from £3 to £20.

Crepe shawls, marvellous specimens of knitting, in the same quality of wool as the very fine lace shawls but in a plain knit pattern, were also on offer. Their very plainness tested the knitter, since each fine stitch had to be correct to achieve overall evenness of texture. Motoring scarves and neckties cost 8s to 40s, the lacier the dearer. Clouds, long scarves knitted in garter stitch and gathered and tassled at either end, were yet another fashion. Circular and square veils were also sold in this department, although the illustration is of a semi-circular veil knitted in the bird's eye pattern.

Precise measurements were requested by the underwear department, but, should this not be possible, details of the wearer's height and whether they be stout or slender are requested. Vests, socks, drawers, gloves, belts and spencers in summer and winter weights were available for babies, children, men and women. There was a large choice in each category.

Waistcoats, machine knitted in double thread, were offered as a motoring speciality. Even knee-cap warmers came in two styles. Vests and undervests, special caps to be worn beneath more fashionable bonnets were all sold to keep winter's chill at bay.

Children could be wrapped in abdominal and cholera belts and overalls, which were long drawers and booties in one.

Spencers came with high or low necks, with or without sleeves, waisted or not. This garment was worn over a waistcoat or for evening wear as an undervest. Being light, usually four to nine ounces, its small space made it specially useful under uniforms. The porous and elastic qualities of Shetland wool helps garments adapt to the shape of the wearer. In the late 1970s coloured spencers in jumper yarn were sold by Shetland firms as fashion garments.

Fair Isle goods received a special chapter. Caps, cowls, cravats, socks and gloves, priced from 3s in 'quaint moorish patterns which were brought out in dark Indian red, buttercup yellow, blue indigo and seal brown with very rich effects'. Mention is made of the flagship of the Spanish Armada which, under the command of the Duke of Medina Sidonia, was driven

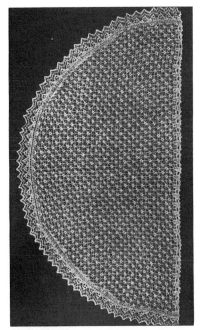

Shetland veil.   Spencer.

F.I. Tam o'Shanter.

8

ashore on Fair Isle in 1588. The Spanish seamen were said to have taught the islanders the art of natural dying using local plants.

Scotch woollen goods were also on offer and one could purchase a Greenlander or Icelander cap, a Tam o' Shanter and even rabbit wool gloves.

Various styles of socks and stockings, special gout stockings and footless stockings — leggings worn with knickerbockers — were offered to the fashionable gent. At a charge of 9d extra, double toes and heels could be added. Gloves, too, came in many guises. Wrist warmers, gauntlets and bag gloves, with separated thumbs suitable for shooting. A special hole for the trigger finger to pop out could be made at no extra charge.

A man is pictured in a cowl and cravat, illustrating the adaptable knitted sausage that could be wrapped round your neck or pulled onto your head to make a snug cap.

I shall pass over the chapters on tweed or claith, blankets and rugs. Interesting as they are they have little bearing on the main purpose of this book.

The Edwardian patrons of this establishment were requested to order by letter or telegram, and orders over 10s were sent post free in Britain and Ireland. When returning goods, however, there was a request that a separate letter be sent in advance. Customer files were kept detailing

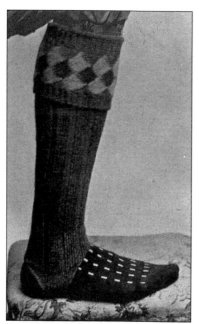

Footless stockings.

Cowl and cravat.

previous orders and noting temporary or summer addresses. New customers had to send cash with order.

Scotch and Shetland spinning wheels were available for £3 and 36s respectively, while a Shetland spinney cost only 30s. Reels, winders, carding combs as well as old wheels and a repair service were available.

Once the carded wool, at 7s 6d a pound, was spun it could be knitted on steel wires at 1d for four or Vulcanite needles at 6d a pair. Steel wires are still preferred by many Shetland women and adverts appear in local shop windows and the local paper announcing their arrival. Knitting patterns were sent post free or you could delve into a book by Patons of Knitting and Crochet Receipts by Mrs Scrivenor, with over a hundred illustrations at a cost of 1s.

Savings could be made by ordering from the cheap goods department.

Good customer relations must have been a priority, for a large setion on washing and aftercare of garments comes at the end of the catalogue. Underclothing should be washed in two or three ounces of good, plain yellow soap boiled down in a little water. In areas of hard water washing soda may be added. Several rinses and no rubbing is recommended, and garments should be dried flat, preferably weighted on top. To finish off, the garment should be ironed under a sheet of calico and finally aired in front of a slow fire, as too fierce a heat could mean shrinkage.

Customers were begged, in capital letters, to send fine lace work to the experts. The cleaning and dressing department guaranteed no shrinkage and quick service. Wednesday was washing day, so no garment took longer than eight days to be returned. This service was fairly cheap with 1½d for a pair of socks to 2s for a shawl. Ten days was all it took for last year's white shawl to be dyed wine, black or scarlet and at only 2s 6d this seems a bargain. White garments were treated with sulphur fumes to whiten and disinfect them. Many knitters and shops in Shetland today still wash and repair shawls and allovers for customers.

Would that today's mail order catalogues were half as interesting. Many folk must have had pleasure and comfort from their purchases. Until recently a similar establishment stood only a street away from this original store.

Spencers, shawls and lace are still knitted and sold but today's knitwear is represented more by patterned garments. Fair Isle is used to describe most of this work but such patterns are knitted throughout the Shetland Isles. The following chapters describe and illustrate the rich history of knitwear and traditions of the knitters of Shetland.

FAIR ISLE

In his essay 'Random Memories — The Coast of Fife' Robert Louis Stevenson describes Fair Isle thus: "Halfway between Orkney and Shetland, there lies a certain isle, on one hand the Atlantic, on the other the North Sea bombard its pillard cliffs; sore-eyed, short-living, inbred fishers and their families herd in few huts; in the graveyard pieces of wreckwood stand for monuments; there is nowhere a more inhospitable spot. Belle-isle-en-Mer — Fair Isle at Sea — that is a name that always runs in my mind's ear like music, but the only fair isle on which I ever set foot, was this unhomely rugged turret top of submarine sierras.'

He goes on to tell of the El Gran Griffin, flagship of the Spanish Armada, whose sailors were harboured for long months by the islanders. He notes that the folk of the northern isles are all 'great artificers of knitting', but only the Fair Islanders dye their fabric in the Spanish manner. Mention was also made that decorated, knitted gloves and night caps were sold on Fair Isle in the catechist's house.

Today we cannot better Stevenson's somewhat dramatic description on the geography of Fair Isle, but perhaps 'the island of sheep' from the Norse describes more accurately this isolated isle. The folk are busy, prosperous and kindly. It is remote but one could not describe the life as dull, — perhaps a bit idyllic, although that may also be its attraction. Of the inhabitants, few are Shetlanders far less true Fair Islanders. The mixture seems to work, incomers bringing skills and talents to help the island's economy.

An air service tempts visitors to this bird-watcher's paradise and offers the locals an alternative to the ferry boat, at present the Good Shepherd IV, which crosses the Roost in all weathers taking cargo, livestock and passengers to the Shetland Mainland.

For over 400 years the islanders have knitted, and travellers tell of knitted gloves and stockings in variegated colours being sold to visitors or used for barter.

In the last twenty years of the 1800s the women started to knit allover patterned jerseys and trade was good until after World War I when fashions changed. To help the declining industry the Shetland Wool Board asked the then Prince of Wales (later Edward VIII) to wear a Fair Isle jumper and this he did. It should be stressed, however, that his garment was knitted on the Shetland Mainland and not in Fair Isle, but nevertheless a fashion trend was established.

Hand-spinning died out during the first world war, and after 1920 more jumpers were knitted in natural colours with patterns spaced farther apart. Between the wars most work was sent to shops in Lerwick or Orkney and there exchanged for goods. The truck system, abolished in the last century, was still practised in the islands and, if money was requested, only 8d or 9d in the shilling was offered. The Second World

11

Old F.I. knitter.   *Shetland trade mark.*

War brought orders from the forces for small items, but demand outweighed supply.

Genuine Fair Isle knitwear carried a special trade mark. Knitters, aged 17 or over, could present work to a committee of three isleswomen who judged the quality of the garment. If suitable, a woven label was sewn onto the garment by machine. This point is curious; to qualify for the trademark every part of the garment had to be handknitted, yet the row of obvious white machine stitching at the back neck of the jersey did mislook it. This trade mark no longer exists, although the Shetland Island's Council have recently introduced a trademark to indentify genuine Shetland knitwear.

Natural dying is a complicated and sometimes unpredictable business. Books have been written about the various plants and techniques used to achieve the soft, yet intense colours quite different to those given by manufactured dyes. In late summer and early autumn the islanders gathered the ripened plants and prepared to dye the year's wool supply. Hanks of unbleached white wool were used with alum as a mordant (colour fixative). The local plants and mosses give various shades of yellow, brown and orange; indigo was bought to give blue and madder for red. Green yarn required to be dyed first yellow, possibly using a local plant called blocks (marsh marigold) and then dyed blue.

Old garment at bird observatory.

Anne Sinclair.

Child's scarf.

13

Because of the extra work involved green was not commonly used. Today, like spinning, natural dying is practised for interest but it is many years since naturally dyed garments were sold commercially. More information on Shetland dying recipes is available in Ursula Venables' 'Life in Shetland' and in 'A Shetland Dye Book' by Jenni Simmons.

The Fair Isle Bird Observatory has a small display of old Fair Isle knitwear and, pinned to the beams of the dining-room are long two colour samplers of Fair Isle and Shetland patterns knitted by Perry Barnes in the 1960s.

Anne Sinclair of Busta showed me three pieces of old Fair Isle knitwear. A child's scarf, bought in Orkney, possibly at Rendall's Shop, about 60 years ago, was knitted in hap weight wool using a very tight tension — 25½ loops (stitches) and 23 rows to two inches. Wires used were size 124 and the wool was home dyed on a white background. Both ends of the scarf were open with short thin tassles knotted all around.

The second piece was a man's dark fawn V-neck allover. The V-neck on this sweater and also on a more recent sleeveless slipover by Agnes Stout were unlike any I have seen elsewhere.

The final piece, a hat around 100 years old known as a 'haaf cap', and similar in shape to a nightcap was worn by fishermen. In the Lerwick Museum there is a double thickness reversible haaf cap, the fancy pattern being worn ashore and the simpler side worn at sea. Anne, a folk singer, tells that fishermen were identified by the haaf caps on the bodies washed ashore after a fishing disaster.

The wool used for the old knitwear was much thinner than is used

Haaf cap.

Old F.I. jumper.

14

Two examples of allovers.

today. Most Shetland jumpers, hats and gloves are knitted in two ply Shetland wool which is similar in weight to four ply wool from general wool shops. Shetland three ply is similar to double knitting and lace yarn is like a normal two ply. Machine spun one ply wool, which only comes in white is about the thickness of sewing cotton.

On the Mainland I was told that the traditional patterns and their position on a garment were symbolic; but the islanders shook their heads at yet another myth. Some patterns had names — Ram's Horns, Creepy Legs (a creepy is a small stool), Armada Closs — but many have several common names, and others are referred to by the name of the knitter who passed it on — 'Mrs Robertson's Star' for example. The older handknitters still keep many patterns 'in their heads' but graph books of patterns are kept for reference. Border patterns are referred to as 'grunds' and larger patterns as 'flo'ers'. A fivey flo'er is pattern set on fives. No one knows the origins of the patterns and they are accepted as traditional, but anyone with an eye for design must note the similarity with patterns from Turkey and the East. The gift of a kaleidoscope, at the turn of the century, again added variations. All genuine Fair Isle patterns are banded around garments whereas elsewhere in Shetland vertical panels or a continuous overall design are knitted.

An Unst minister, visiting Fair Isle in the early part of the century, bought patterned jumpers to take back for the women of Unst to copy. Patterns went to the Ness (south Mainland) in the same way, and thus the patterns moved round Shetland.

Today handknitters on Fair Isle are few, but April 7th, 1980 saw

15

Old piece of knitwear as memory aid.

F.I. hat and scarf.

Sampler.

the birth of Fair Isle Crafts — a knitting co-operative — backed by both the Shetland Islands Council and the Highlands and Islands Development Board. There are 12 members including two husband and wife teams, and most are aged 25-40 with young families. All the work is carried out in the member's homes using Knitmaster punch card machines capable of two colour knitting. Some members knit, others hand finish the garments, dress and dispatch them, or attend to the paper work. The co-operative aims to encourage knitters to express individuality in their work, new ideas and colour schemes are welcomed and although the range is limited it covers jumpers, slipovers, hats, scarves, legwarmers and samplers. Summer visitors can attend a weekly workshop where a knitter and finisher demonstrate and answer questions. Finished work and sample swatches are on display and orders taken. Handknitters may be visited at home where unusual and attractive souvenirs, such as tea-cosies with Fair Isle knitted into them or egg-cosies decorated with 'peerie patterns', can be bought reasonably cheaply.

Prince Phillip and the late King Olaf of Norway were presented with handknitted allovers made by Annie Thomson of the Post Office during their visit to Shetland in May 1981.

Ann Prior who was cooking for the summer season at the Bird Observatory when I stayed there, had spun thick yarn from local fleeces, and knitted this, using the bolder Fair Isle patterns, into unusual chunky sweaters. Most local knitters were keen to try out new ideas and we saw several fine landscape sweaters depicting local views.

The National Trust for Scotland own Fair Isle and have reproduced the patterns on a range of tin ware. The islanders produce stoneware mugs with Fair Isle transfers and the Shetland Workshop Gallery in Lerwick published cards depicting Fair Isle patterns. Other commercial firms use the motifs on various goods and perhaps the ideas could be expanded by non-knitting craftsmen on Fair Isle.

A Fair Isle jumper, like an Arran sweater or a Guernsey, is a classic, and the part-time knitters of the island have a limited production so there will never be a glut of genuine Fair Isle jumpers. The mass-produced copies, by the Scottish mills and the imported Fair Isles from Taiwan, although cheap, will never appeal to the purist who not only purchases a sweater but the tradition and history of many years.

Left:
Tea cosy.

Right:
Egg cosy.

F.I. Allover

Anne Prior's thick knit.

F.I. Post Office.

18

Landscape jumper.

Allover.

UNST

Imagine a giant cobweb and you are probably picturing nature's version of one of the beautiful, handspun Unst shawls. In this, the most northerly of Britain's isles, the women spun and knitted delicate lace and have become world famous for the quality of their work.

Although as an industry this died out during the First World War, when knitters turned their hands to producing gravets and body belts for the troops, it is continued today as a craft on a small scale, more for interest than profit. Mary Jane Peterson of Muness is the only remaining spinner of the very fine lace yarn and she has won many prizes for her work. A shawl knitted in her own spun yarn has recently been purchased by the Scottish Development Agency for inclusion in its Scottish Crafts Collection.

In former days most crofts had a spinning wheel; on this 'swara', the rough wool used to knit socks and workclothes for the family, was spun. The spinners of the fine lace yarn had a second wheel kept solely for the purpose of spinning lace weight wool. Generally the fine yarn was spun in the south of Unst and the lace knitting done in the north. The expression 'going to the shore' describes the walk to Uyeasound, in the south, to purchase yarn from the merchant who built his shop near the shore, since boats were the most common form of transport. The spinners sold their yarn to the shop and knitters purchased it from the merchant at prices varying from 3d per 100 threads for coarser lace, to 6d for very fine wool. Considering earnings at this time the fine yarn cost a great deal. Since all the yarn was not produced by one spinner knitters had to spend time comparing thickness and qualities before work commenced.

Mary Jane Peterson.

Handspun very fine lace.

21

Apart from lace stoles, scarves and shawls the women knitted veils and triangular head scarves. Silk triangular veils, knitted with the eyelid pattern, were worn over the face and wrapped around a hat, and veils in fine black, white and moorit spun yarn could be folded and fitted into a matchbox. In the 1800s very fine silk thread was rolled in flour to help knitters see their work.

In recent years several brides have worn fine shawls as wedding veils, but on enquiring if this was an Unst fashion folk could only remember one bride veiled this way. Past trends show brides dressed in blue or white, and it was customary to wear your wedding dress at future weddings to bring luck. The best maid, however, wore a new outfit. We saw a fine stole in 2 ply handspun lace, knitted for a bride by her mother, and worn on her wedding day in March 1932 when the wedding procession walked from the kirk to the reception. The same lady showed us a shawl measuring 1¾ yards square weighing a mere 3½ ounces and a stole 72 inches by 26 inches weighing 1½ ounces. The fineness of this work enables even large shawls to be pulled through a wedding ring.

Today T. M. Hunter of Brora spin a fine 1 ply lace wool, but this is more similar in appearance and texture to fine cotton. The handspun yarn was delicate and soft, often finer than a strand of hair. Some folk recalled a commercial spinner, perhaps Munro, producing a very fine 2 ply yarn.

In the late fifties and early sixties classes in fine spinning were taught by a lady then in her seventies. Local women supplied their own wheels. The teacher received a letter from H. M. Queen Elizabeth, the Queen Mother, thanking her for keeping alive this traditional craft. At the age of 80 this same lady was still knitting and spinning work of a quality to again interest the Royal Family, when Princess Margaret purchased a scarf at the Royal Highland Show in Aberdeen.

A set of three lace doillies knitted in crochet cotton, as a wedding gift in 1920, and a tray cloth, made from No. 10 cotton, which the present owner had starched with cornflour, were part of a collection of lace that Barry Spence of Millburn had assembled for an exhibition of lace. She also had a beautiful nightdress bag which was unlined so the colour of the nightgown peeped through the lace holes. This was knitted in the e'ed lace. Many lace patterns appeared in variations and one knitter is said to have six different versions of the print and the wave, but the one that intrigued me most was 'the puzzle'. Merino yarn from Australia, was knitted into a stole by an old lady from Pediser and this too was in Barry's collection. It was much fluffier than Shetland lace wool.

In 1933 or '34 Mrs Ann Johnston of Seaview, Baltasound, won first prize in a Daily Mail competition. Her entry was an evening purse and shawl. Seven natural colours, from white through fawns to moorit, were knitted into the border and the branch or madeira patterns were used. The matching purse was lined with silk.

Prizewinning shawl.

Barry Spence.

Another unusual shawl was called a spotted hap. Unfortunately at the time it was incomplete, the knitter making it from memory to sell at the local sale of work. These haps were originally knitted in grey or moorit with white. The spotted effect used in the centre of the hap was also knitted in children's socks, nightcaps and gloves. This was the first time I had seen this design.

Crochet, in the fine lace yarn, does not seem to have been popular. One schoolteacher, however, taught the girls in her class to make 'peerie bits o' lace to trim their unmentionables'.

Spun silk had at one time been knitted into stockings and we were told of a French lady who ordered lace jabots, which she fastened with a brooch at the neck of her costume. This was the second reference to French ladies, the other being the wife of a knitwear merchant in Lerwick at the turn of the century; one wonders if French style ever influenced the Shetland knitwear trade.

Spinning classes are still taught during the winter months. Local women, interested in the old skills, not only spin but many knit up the fine yarn into scarves and stoles. A Professor Drever of St Andrews collected musk wool off the craigs during a visit to the Arctic region of Canada and had it spun in Unst. The wool was similar in colour to 'shaella', a pinkish fawn. The same spinner also spun dog hair, of a

23

mauvish shade, and the resulting yarn was made into a rug and presented to a university.

Although the fine lace work gave way to Fair Isle as the most common form of knitting, women continued to make lace scarves. During the Second World War, when the pension was only 10s, knitters could sell as many scarves as they could produce for the princely sum of 10s.

The older knitters said that Fair Isle knitting arrived in Unst around the time of the First World War, and a Mr Erland Sandison, who had tearooms at Baltasound, was spoken of by many as being in the forefront of this trade. A woman recalled her sister knitting the first Fair Isle garment for Mr Sandison, copying a sample and improving on it. It was a long sleeved V-neck allover, extra long in the body and patterned all over with red, gold, blue and wheat on a moorit background. He paid 12s for the garment and supplied the wool. He sold one-off designs as well, and most of his jumpers had bands of patterns, large and small designs alternating. His business lasted until the early 1940s.

In 1924 the first prize for the county was given to Edie, one of the Sutherland sisters, for a panelled Fair Isle jumper in white with blues and golds, which was purchased by Professor Jamieson of Edinburgh. This was one of the first panelled jumpers to be seen. A photo of Edie as a young girl shows her wearing a scoop neck jersey made on Fair Isle with a matching knee-length skirt, knitted in the kiltie-pleat — a stylish outfit in its day. Much mention was made of knitted skirts. Some were ribbed, others, especially childrens' ones, were knitted in the kiltie-pleat and a more recent design was a 3 ply skirt with shaped panels, one plain and the next in diagonal rib. This skirt had a jacket to match. Suits are always fashionable, and little girls wore skirts in one colour with a

One of the Sutherland sisters in old Fair Isle scarf and close ups.

Old allover and close up.

contrasting top trimmed in Fair Isle to match the skirt. Little boys, too, had knitted outfits. One lad, photographed around 1926, posed in knitted trousers and a Fair Isle border jersey. This small Fair Isle trim was referred to by his grandmother as a 'poverty strip'.

In the 1920s long plain jumpers with large sailor collars in brown or moorit edged in white were knitted and sold to a William Mouat. Yet another style, known as frocks, were made from two heads of jumpers yarn. They had a rib skirt, low waist, plain body and a V-neck. The waist and cuffs had a Fair Isle band as decoration. Mr Humphries of Uyeasound paid 15s a piece for these frocks. At this time scarves were very long and about 14 or 15 inches wide. Old photographs show ladies and gentlemen of the day fashionably attired thus on the golf course or on country weekends.

By the time the Second World War came fashions had changed, nevertheless the forces, stationed in the isles, bought a little, and demand always outweighed supply. A spencer normally cost 7s 6d, but a RAF man, stationed at Skaw, was paying 16s for them. Patterned spencers, with the print and wave over the breast and a shell edging were knitted on the island and sold to the more genteel clothing stores in London.

A Glasgow lady, who had best remain nameless, and who for her own reasons, — perhaps tax avoidance or something more intriguing — resided at ever-changing addresses, kept the Unst women busy knitting Fair Isle berets. She paid 7s 6d each and one lady supposedly knitted four berets a day, but I think she must have burned the midnight oil from time to time. Still this was good extra cash during the war years.

Hats in the past eighty years have changed with the whims of fashion. Knitted hats such as berets, pillboxes, skull caps, beanies, toories, bonnets and Sumburgh bonnets a great fashion of the early sixties similar to a Fair Isle baseball cap and worn by golfers and sportswomen have been made by the women of Shetland. Theodora Coutts of Lerwick, who was a well known knitwear designer produced a version of a deerstalker with Fair Isle patterns. Unst women talked of a style of hat, similar to a nightcap fastened at the side with a tassle which was worn by them to school in their youth. They also knitted large Fair Isle Tam o' Shanters with long tassles. Gladys Gjerde, one of the best knitters I have met, deserves a mention, especially for the crowns on her hats which are unique. Where most Shetland hats have a large star on the crown to incorporate the very intricate intaking that shapes the hat, she has diamonds and trees and twists — all beautifully blended to match the patterns used in the hat. Her tips on shading colours were to keep the background dark or medium dark and change colours where the pattern broadens out. On a seventeen row pattern colours used would be 3,3,2,1,2,3,3, with a centre row picked out in a sharp or contrasting colour like the stamen of a flower.

In 1963, with the twin aims of providing a better price for the knitter and a more interesting garment for the customer, June Owers, niece of the aforementioned Mr Sandison, set up her 'knittery' which ran successfully for the next seventeen years. She started Skerry Knitwear with one girl who had completed a knitting machine training course at Keith. Most of the garments were knitted in pieces and linked together.

Fully fashioned knitwear is not usually the norm in Shetland and only latterly did this firm produce seamfree garments. Most designs were based on yoked garments. Three depths of yokes were produced from 3 inch to a deep yoke of 9 inches. V-neck cardigans and fisher-ribs were also knitted with yoked designs. The Norwegian Star pattern was knitted on a bleached white background with no background shading, tones of the body colour were used instead of a contrasting shade in the star. A pattern, known as the pagoda, was often used in place of the trees which is the traditional pattern used to intake and shape the yoke between the stars. Occasionally a complex chain or an anchor pattern is used for this purpose. Another design had a panel of Fair Isle down the front of the jumper, often the Cunningsburgh pattern, or two small panels either side of the buttons on a mandarin collar lumber jacket. These panels should be knitted at a tighter tension so the knitting does not sag. The knitters were very involved in this business and each year new designs

A selection of hats.

were tried out and colour combinations changed, then added to an evergrowing repertoire of styles. Often ideas had to be rejected as too difficult or time-consuming, or because Shetland wool will not hold the shape of too complex a style.

Allover Fair Isle socks, to be worn with knickerbockers, were produced. The patterned cuff turned over a band of ribbing and the leg and top of the foot were also knitted in Fair Isle, the sole being 1 X 1 rib. Ribbed stockings with a Fair Isle cuff were knitted for the less flamboyant gent. Socks, knitted around Whiteness and Weisdale, in rather more feminine shades were worn by sporting ladies in the twenties and two pairs I own and a couple of pairs I have seen were knitted flat and sewn up on the inside. Socks with Fair Isle patterns were still knitted recently by an Unst lady and sold for skiing.

Various parts of Shetland had their own patterns, but today with the ease of travel, most patterns are knitted in most areas. A design known as the Whalsay pattern was used on a sweater for Sir Winston Churchill

Traditional Unst allover.

and henceforth became known as the Churchill pattern.

A former fashion, perhaps due for revival, was a twinset with a Fair Isle trimmed cardigan worn over a short sleeved allover, the borders being a repeat of one of the patterns on the allover.

We were shown no silk knitwear with Fair Isle designs on Unst. This is one fashion of which there are few remaining garments. I saw a photograph of a 1920s flapper dress in silk with a Fair Isle bodice, and

Allovers from Unst.

a waistcoat knitted in wool with silk patterns on it. This garment was knitted for a Whalsay man and is still worn by his daughter.

Children, as elsewhere on the islands, were taught to knit at an early age. One lady recalled knitting her own stockings to hang up for Santa Claus at Old Christmas. Auld Yule which falls on the 6th of January and the Auld New Year a week later are still celebrated in parts of Shetland, indeed both old and new are celebrated in some places.

At Baltasound School in 1922 or '23 the teacher, a Mrs Hunter, had her pupils printing pattern books of Fair Isle designs, which were then sold. The blunt end of a matchstick was dipped in red, blue, green and black ink and dotted onto graph paper. These sound similar to the books produced by Mr Williamson of Lerwick.

White wool today can be bought bleached or unbleached and 'Superwhite' or some similar product is often used to brighten up a garment that has yellowed with age or too much sunlight. Until the early sixties, however, people still used brimstone to whiten garments and yarn. The item was first washed twice and rinsed, then a smoking barrel was prepared. An iron pot or crock was used and a red hot peat coal was placed in the bottom. Two clean sticks were placed across the top and the garment hung over them. This was covered with a clean sheet or towel and topped by a thick coat or blanket. Rock sulphur was added and the barrel closed. After four hours the garment was taken out, shaken, and the process repeated. One rinse in lukewarm water was given and a little 'blue' and small amount of starch, depending on the weight of the garment, was added. Shawls would be strung up beforehand so

29

that they could be stretched out straight away to dry on a frame. When stretchers were not available the shawl would be pinned out over a clean white sheet on the grass to dry. Stretching or 'dressing' a garment is most important and special boards are used to dry berets, scarves, jumpers, socks, spencers, gloves and mitts. Berets are dried on dinner plates and hats shaped over pudding basins. The stretching of lace is very important as this gives the knitting the gossamer appearance.

What else do these enterprising knitters of the north make? We saw borders of ducks, silhouetted swallows and even a yoke of roses. The most unusual lace item we saw was definitely a pair of lace curtains — and large curtains at that — knitted in 'Oh So Silky' yarn to a pattern that had appeared in a woman's magazine.

At the 1949 exhibition at Alexandra Palace, London, Unst women demonstrated fine lace spinning and knitting, both Fair Isle and lace. Women from Shetland go all over the world demonstrating their craft at trade shows and in store promotions. Let us hope that for many more years they have a craft left to represent.

Above: Yoke of roses.

Left: Silk and wool waistcoat.

SKERRIES

The trip to Skerries is not to be forgotten. Three hours in a small, cold boat with black skies and tossing seas is not my idea of travelling in comfort, so as the pier lights of Skerries came into view I looked forward to my four nights on dry land.

Wind and rain greeted us but the pier was crowded with folk collecting their errands and hearing the news. A strong impression of Skerries is a constant bustle rather than the 'manyana' existence of so many remote communities.

Three small islands form the Skerries group. The east and west isles are linked by a short bridge and Grunay, recently with a population of two but now uninhabited, is reached by a short trip in a rowing boat.

Because of the safe anchorages fishing is important, with three working fishing boats and a fish factory now used for grading and processing salmon. With this income and additional earnings from crofting and knitting, the industrious islanders are fairly prosperous. They have

Tom Bogle in traditional allover.

31

not given up, to live on past memories and dole cheques, but are very much a community of the nineties.

The soil cover is sparse, and at the turn of the century, when most families crofted, every small area of good land was under cultivation. Crops were grown, sheep reared and, when possible, an in-milk cow and young calf kept. The islesmen fished, in summer landing herring at Lerwick or packing fish in ice to be shipped to Aberdeen. In the winter they went to the haddock, in small boats using long lines, the cleaning and baiting of which were, like net-mending, carried out between trips by the women and older children, using limpets and mackerel as bait.

Women ran the croft as well as the home, filling the long days of summer with outdoor tasks. While carrying home kishies of peats or leading the cow to new pastures they knitted on short wires, which did not need the support of a knitting belt, lengths of hap lace, the pique edging for shawls, or made socks. A hank of wool was carried over the arm or a ball of yarn in the pinny pocket. Many old pictures show knitters thus. Most raw wool was carded and spun in summer so a large supply was ready for winter. The days of winter were short and outside chores fewer, the women gathered around the peat fire to knit, oil and later gas lamps supplying additional light.

Simple styles in natural-coloured homespun yarn were worn at home — knitted haps and stockings by the women, with special thick socks to wear with rivlins, the hide shoes which wrapped over the feet and laced up the legs. Sealskin rivlins were said to be more comfortable than

Three schoolgirls in yokes.

32

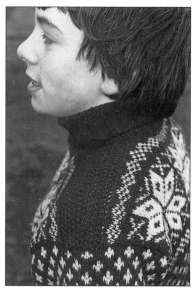

Above: Simple allover with patterned yoke.

Right: Detailed shoulder strap for extending life of jumper by enabling wearer to wear it back to front.

those in cowhide. Men wore navy or Shetland black, plain jerseys sometimes with a textured pattern such as the honeycomb, across the chest to give extra thickness and warmth. Their socks were also handknitted, with special thick, long socks to wear under the long, leather seaboots. Mufflers were used to tie up the few possessions that accompanied them on sea trips. Black and white dice mittens, with set-in thumbs for less restricted movements, were worn to pack fish in ice. The pattern was of little import, the simple two colour design enabling two strands of wool to be used and double the thickness of the mitts. Re-footing socks, patching and darning were all women's work that had to be completed before knitting for profit could begin. Hardly profit, as the work was badly paid, but still even a little extra helped.

The local merchant at this time was an Alec Humphries. He seems to have been well respected and paid the sum of 1s 6d per spencer, although as usual the payment was made in goods. One woman was given an extra 3d to encourage her as she was 'just a young lass'. Nine shillings was paid for a man's frock, a short sleeved semmit, knitted in jumper yarn and this princely sum enabled the knitter to buy material to cover two quilts. The same lady told me she was only a child of eleven when she sold six small Fair Isle bordered jumpers to a shop in Whalsay. Fair Isle gloves, berets and tassled nightcaps were also knitted to sell. Around 1918 an allover, made from scraps of left-over wool, and with every pattern different, sold to a Yell merchant for 35s.

Fisher lasses, who spent the summer months at the gutting in

Lerwick, brought pattern books back to Skerries. Old pages, most in tatters, are still to be found in some Shetland households. They were school graph books onto which designs were stamped in red and green with the words 'genuine Fair Isle' stamped across the corner of each page. They came in three volumnes and cost half a crown each. Mr Robbie Williamson, who ran a bicycle shop on the stretch of Commercial Street to the south of the Market Cross, is said to have printed and sold these books. He had a hairdresser's shop in his back room, a bicycle shop downstairs and, across the road, a photographer's studio. Next door to this was another interesting shop — Old Angus's — a bookshop which also sold yellow dusters and had a monopoly on the supply of Typhoo Tea. Patterns from Mr Williamson's books appear in the pattern section at the end of this book.

The first knitting machines arrived on Skerries in the 1930s, one of which was a sock machine. Machine ribs benefit the handknitter, saving time and providing a firmer more elastic rib. Allovers are often made with a shaded 1 x 1 or 2 x 2 rib, some knitters believing these basques last longer and frame the multi-colour garment more effectively.

In 1940 one family knitted a regular order, received by an Aunt from a lady in London for cardigans, worn as part of a school uniform. Each dark fawn cardigan had a blue Fair Isle trim above the basque and cuffs and were worn by girls of eight to ten. 7s 6d was paid for each completed garment.

The school pupils, dressed in two colour allovers of forty years ago, were probably not too different from today's children. Apart from the vivid colours of today's sweaters the main difference in allovers was the

Skerries schoolbairns.

Skerries allover.

Bovril jumper.

Skerries schoolbairns.

predominance of panelled jumpers rather than the banded designs of the past. Shaded colours became more fashionable after the last war. The bairns we met were all attired in spectacular jumpers of yellow and blue, turquoise and white, and one knitted in red and black known as the Bovril jumper. OXO is a fairly common name for various Fair Isle patterns but why Bovril? One answer was that both products were similar as were the patterns, the other theory was that the shape of the Bovril bottle is similar to the pattern casing.

Scotch wool and Shetland 3 ply, which is equivalent to the thickness of double knitting yarn, was used in many of the jumpers worn by the folk themselves, although jumper weight 2 ply jumpers are still knitted to sell. Square yokes were popular and a cardigan fastened with metal clips and trimmed with fancy braid copied the style of Norwegian cardigans popular with the Shetlanders in the late sixties. Lace and Fair Isle combined in one garment was another idea that had been tried, but this is rarely a successful combination. In recent years lace yokes with shaded colours in a shell pattern knitted onto machine made bodies were popular with the women of Shetland. Embroidered jumpers, a style popular in the fifties, were also produced on Skerries. Pansies and twisted flowers can still occasionally be seen on knitwear in the Lerwick shops.

Fisherman's gansies were, and are, worn all over Britain. The most famous, the Guernsey, and of course the intricate sweaters from the Arran Islands of Ireland are now the garb of sportsmen and townsfolk alike, and when in Skerries I was shown a Shetland version of this garment. Although these sweaters are traditionally knitted in navy blue the one I saw was in light blue with raised patterns of waves, ropes and basket stitch.

Skerries Norwegian copy.

Fisherman's gansie.

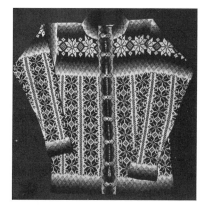

Clockwise from above:
T. Goudie Norwegian influence,
T. Goudie Norwegian influence.
Squared yoke allover.
Squared yoke.

The primary schoolchildren had visited the island's knitters to research a project on knitting in Skerries. One lady told them that as a young girl she was given a spinning wheel. It was brought back from Norway for her by her father and was painted with spots of red, blue and mustard with the words "spin spin dötter min' on the pedal.

Many variations of the Norwegian Star and some similarity to the Faroese patterns appeared on the knitwear. A lumber jacket, in naturals with a touch of RAF blue, worn by the then headmaster's wife Pat, had been copied from a Norwegian knitting leaflet. Incidentally the pamphlet cover shows a cap similar to a haaf cap. Many of the patterns on this knitting graph are the same as those in traditional Shetland knitting. A chain has been added to the pattern set to lengthen the garment.

'Start no work on Fridays', 'Don't knit to a fisherman on Helly days and Yule', 'If someone enters the room quickly when you are laying up a jumper then it will be quickly finished', these are some quoted knitting superstitions of the islands.

Knitting sheaths, made of gulls feathers bound with braid in fancy patterns, or wrapped in oilcloth, were remembered but none still existed, having been replaced by modern knitting belts in leather or sealskin.

Raw wool, for shipment to T. M. Hunter of Brora, was accepted at both the east and west isle shops. Crofters could receive cash or spun yarn in return. Today, wool is only a small part of the huge range of merchandise for sale in both shops. Although a new roll-on, roll-off ferry has replaced the Spes Clara the Skerries folk do not venture to the Mainland that often.

Today's knitters work on private orders for the south and abroad, supplying shops in Lerwick or doing piece-work for the Mainland factories, and so are still a relevant part of the Skerries economy. Those who do not need the cash knit for 'pin money' and it is traditional that Shetland women do not like to have their hands idle.

Like Gulliver' Lilliputia, Skerries had it all — cliffs, hills, moors and seascapes, all in miniature but all enchanted. On the last night of my visit there was a display of the Northern Lights, a fitting end to a magical stay in a magic land.

Copy of Norwegian lumber.

Private order from Skerries.

FETLAR

Fetlar is a small, pretty isle to the east of Yell, with fine sandy beaches and, in summer, banks of wild flowers that give it the title 'the garden of Shetland'. About 100 folk live on the island, much smaller than past populations, but many of the inhabitants are very young, and a new scheme to encourage incomers is now in operation. Folk croft and knit for the larger factories on the Mainland.

Until World War II the island held an annual agricultural show where knitwear as well as produce and livestock was judged. Today, much of the fertile land is uncultivated and it would appear that most of Fetlar's glory is in the past.

The traditional knitting of Fetlar was similar to that of Unst, the women spinning and knitting fine lace scarves and shawls. The local merchant bought the homespun yarn and a little knitting, but most work

Prizewinning V-neck allover.

39

was sold to the Mid Yell shop. Women took their wares over on the small rowing boat that carried the mail to the islanders. Later the inter island steamer, Earl of Zetland, carried parcels to the Lerwick shops, but the Fetlar folk visited the capital rarely, perhaps once a year. Today's roll-on roll-off service via Yell enables the islesfolk to load up with goods in Lerwick and drive them door to door.

Cars were few, and like children all over Shetland, the Fetlar bairns walked to school in all weathers. One woman told me that she had walked from her home in Houll, at the east end of the island daily, a journey of one hour each way. The women remembered their first efforts in knitting. At about five years of age they produced garters for the older relatives and made cradle straps for the younger ones. A cradle strap is a long strip of riggies used to criss cross round the knobs of the cradle so that the sleeping child would not fall out when rocked from side to side. Another woman confessed that knitting had been a real punishment to her and when given the plain fingers to put into gloves she would give them a good pull to the length hoping to stretch her efforts; a pity that wool is so elastic and she always ended up having to knit them to the full length. A knitter recalled that, aged six, she made a plain skull cap, at nine Fair Isle mitts and by fifteen had produced an allover. She desribed it as a navy and white jumper with Norwegian patterns that she assumed had come to Shetland during the Second World War. Several of the women recalled selling children's Fair Isle mitts for pocket money when, as pupils at the Anderson Education Institute in Lerwick, they

Right and wrong sides of sweater.

40

Bairn's mitts.   *Yoke.*

stayed at the school hostel. Most of the isles children and those from the more remote parts of the Mainland stayed at the school hostels or lodged with families in Lerwick. Today the inter-island ferries enable most children to go home every night or at the very least to visit their families each weekend.

No knitting was taught in the island school but ex-pupils said they knitted socks for the soldiers of the First World War and the boys of Fetlar school produced knee warmers, helmets and such for the Red Cross in World War II. This work was arranged by Lady Nicolson of Brough Lodge, the laird's house and buildings that sit on Fetlar's west coast, which even today in their somewhat dilapitated state, are still impressive.

Allover.   *Allover.*

41

Now the pupils of the islands school begin knitting at the age of five, first mastering the techniques of plain knitting and then progressing to work in two colours. For their Fair Isle work the teacher prefers them to use one thread from each hand as she finds this gives a more even texture. In other parts of Shetland knitters hold the wool over two fingers of the right hand and on occasion when three colours are to be knitted in one row the third is held in the left hand. Three colours in one row seems to be more common in older pieces of knitting. The children begin by knitting a bonnet and by the age of nine most have completed a yoke. Their teacher offers the chance to learn knitting to boys but this is usually declined. She also observed that the slowest learner often became the best knitter.

Unlike most other islesmen, the Fetlar men were remembered for their knitting skills. Several folk mentioned Tammy Garriock of Funzie who not only knitted a variety of Fair Isle garments but spun his yarn. His work was remembered as inventive and he won a first prize at the Royal Highland Show.

Few examples of old knitting remained on Fetlar, and I was told that newborn lambs had probably been rolled in the old moth-eaten jumpers. We did see a splendid example of a fashion of thirty years ago, an allover in shades of blue and white. Diamonds were shades from navy through blues to white, and a pattern knitted on the white background; the diamonds were then shaded out again to navy and a pattern set on this. Short zips were often set into necks of sweaters at this time, enabling them to form a collar when unzipped. Another jumper was patterned all over with small diamonds. Inside each diamond was a different design — the star, compass, Whalsay daisy and the butterfly. A Shetland exile,

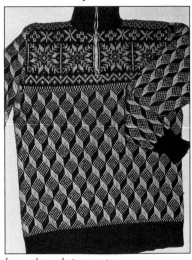

Diamond shaded V-neck.   *Long sleeved zip sweater.*

42

Zip neck open.   *Zip neck closed.*

now resident in Edinburgh knitted similar jumpers. As a young man he was taught to knit to help supplement the family income and although his repertoire was small he produced many garments. Instead of banding his designs around the sweater, he placed them diagonally inside an allover diamond pattern, making a complex and interesting design.

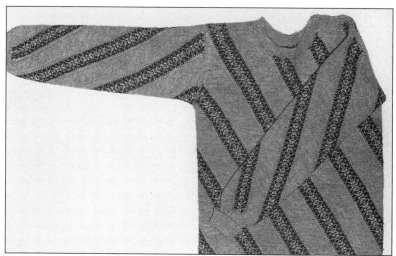

Prizewinning allover knitted in strips.

43

Diamond scarf.

Allover diamonds.

44

Mrs Joan Coutts showed us a most unusual jumper which had won a first prize in 1954 at the Royal Highland Show and several prizes at local arts and crafts competitions. This was a child's jumper, although she had also made an adult version. The plain bands were knitted in dark fawn lace wool. A score of stitches was cast on, and using very fine wires, one stitch was decreased at the beginning of the row and one increased at the end, forming a diagonal strip. Loops were picked up along the edge of this strip and a Fair Isle band, in brown and golds, was then knitted. The next plain strip was grafted on and so the jumper was built up. The idea had first been tried as a scarf.

One last allover is worth a mention, for it was a jumper to fit a 50" chest, with 17 score loops knitted in 3 ply yarn for a special order from south. Not only was it large but very heavy.

A little natural dying had been done in the past, using tea leaves, onion skins, dockenroots and salt and vinegar as setting agents. As in many other areas Fairy and Diamond dyes were used, especially for orange and yellows. Hanks of wool were boiled in a basin on top of the stove and coarse salt added to stop the colour running. It was rare for two dye batches to be the same shade and sometimes the same dye pot was used several times to give paler shades useful in blending and shading patterns.

Recently I heard of a new method of syringe dying where, provided careful notes were kept, the exact shade of wool could be repeated over several batches. Wool that was dyed for me by this method proved to be good and reliable with no colour running when the garment was washed: a good way of achieving colours that are not commercially produced. On a trip to Amsterdam I met a weaver who sold various yarns — wool, flax, cotton, linen and silk — all in a natural shade, and also pots of dye from a Swiss manufacturer that enabled one to choose the exact shade and texture of yarn to knit or weave. This method made for completely unique pieces.

Perhaps the new generation of Fetlar will restore the island's economy and today's schoolchildren may use the technology of the modern knitter to create and invent styles that will be remembered by future generations. Sometimes it is good to look back before going forward.

YELL

Many Yell folk have taken advantage of the regular ferry service to cross the Sound and work on the Mainland, especially at the oil port of Sullom Voe. Those that remain continue to work in much the same way as their forebears — crofting, fishing and knitting.

Much of the island is moorland, the soil poor, and in the past crofters often delled ten acres by hand. The first plough on the island, one man recalled, did not appear until 1917. The coastline is more interesting and of course the sea has always played a big part in the Shetlanders' life. Many men earned their living by going away to sea — fishing, in the merchant service, or to the whaling in South Georgia.

Leaving the island, even for the summer months, meant that money could be earned to help the family income through the long hard winter, and so, many of the young lasses went to the herring gutting in Lerwick.

Yell man in sweater.

Bobby Tulloch.

Work was hard and the hours long, but the camaraderie of the fisher lasses is well known and the women looked forward to meeting friends from former years and re-establishing contact with women from Britain's other coastal areas. Although the gutters bound their fingers with bandages they suffered from sore hands caused by cuts, fish poison and the constant stinging salt, so this and the long hours left little time for handwork apart from mending. Ideas, however, were exchanged and orders for garments to be knitted during the winter were placed. Only if work was slack did their 'sock' appear. Remembering the lack of communications at the time, it must have been stimulating for the isleswomen to hear of the fads and fasions that were popular in the south.

One woman, born in Yell but now resident on the Mainland, said that her mother was one of the first in Yell to knit Fair Isle. She remembered the jumper vividly, it had diamond and cross patterns knitted all over in rust, navy, yellow and red. I asked if she had any pieces of her mother's work but she said they could not afford to keep work and only 'knitted to sell'.

The 1930s style for long Fair Isle trimmed jerseys with crew or V-necks had a Fair Isle border on the neck, cuffs and above the basque. Some had a row of holes knitted above the Fair Isle at the waist and a tassled cord was drawn through this and tied. These garments, which took 1½ to 2 days to knit by hand fetched between 4s 6d and 7s. 'Mind you the pound was a different piece o' paper in those days'. If the body was machine made the time taken was considerably less, but the price paid remained the same. Several Lerwick merchants were producing jumpers thus, and at the same time buying in hand knitted goods. The Shetland Trade Mark was then a Norse Galley, and this was indiscriminately placed by the merchants on all garments. Since the merchants were doing so well at this a Yell man decided to follow suit and purchased a second-hand Dubied knitting machine from Oswald Donner of Kilmarnock for £40. 'A lot o' folk could have cut my throat for it'. He said that many folk were against the introduction of machines believing that they would kill the Shetland knitwear trade.

Coned wool, like we know today, was not available; so wool was run over a household candle to wax it and then wound round a wooden spool.

After the Second World War the 'spivs', as the locals referred to the customs officers began to take an interest in the knitwear trade. The post-war labour government taxed Fair Isle on knitwear as fancy goods at 120%. Ankle hose, in many colours and sizes, with a Fair Isle cuff was affected by this tax. (To get all the gory details we had to switch off the tape recorder). These socks were a good money spinner, as six pairs could be knitted from a head of wool and 24 pairs a day made on a sock machine. Local women were paid half-a-crown to knit on the Fair Isle cuff and, when complete, the hose fetched 10s a pair. Special boards, made from thick ply or cut from old tea chests were used to dress the various sizes of socks. Cash was paid and no records kept.

Crofters often knitted to 'eke oot a living' and they also fished, if not to sell, to feed the family. The description of the Shetlander as 'a fisherman with a croft' used to be given to school children to compare with the Orcadian — 'a farmer with a boat'. Imagine a cold, wet morning, not yet light and the men off to the haddock. When they reach the sea they dip their hands in the sea water and rub hard to prevent the skin from blistering. Then they wring out their woollen gloves or mittens so that the wet salt soaked gloves kept their hands warm. These soaked gloves should end up looking 'as felted as an ox's lug'. At the hand line for profit the men shot four lines of 400 hooks on a trip and in good weather they went off twice a day.

Knitting was not taught in school. Girls learnt at home and one child remembered knitting her first spencer before she went to school, the proceeds from its sale enabled her mother to purchase her first school boots. That same child was knitting Fair Isle jumpers before she was ten and is today still producing beautiful garments. The schoolteacher did, however, turn a 'blind eye' when the exams were over if the girls brought in their knitting to do in their leisure time. This enabled them to finish the work and have a little extra cash over Christmas.

Today's school bairns are taught to knit from the age of five and early on they are taught to make a spencer — properly. It is good to see that the spencer is still considered useful today. Special boards, with hinged centres and straight arms, are used to dress spencers. In Fetlar and Yell people spoke of half boards with only one arm used to stretch spencers. You sewed the spencer double and pulled it on like a sock.

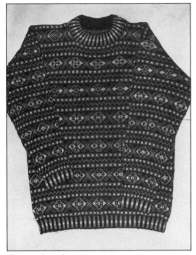

Copy of socks as sweater.   Unusual trimmed V-neck.

Until recently country shops sold special cotton spencer buttons which were soft like liberty bodice buttons.

Some old, rather moth-eaten knitwear was found a few years ago at Park Hall in Mid Yell. Among this were two pairs of rather interesting socks, one, with shaded diamonds and patterns in naturals with green and pink, had Fair Isle heels and on the turn-down cuffs the words FROM SHETLAND knitted. The other pair had stripey toes and heels with traditional patterns and colours. A jumper copying these designs and colours were knitted by Maggie Anne Nicholson of Burravoe. The collection of jumpers at Maggie Anne's house was vast and I found many

Variation on star and tree yoke.

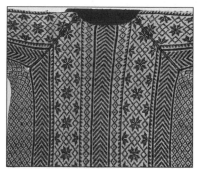

Raglan sleeve.

Raglan sleeve.

Raglan sleeve.

Set in sleeve.

new ideas and patterns. She is an inventive lady copying designs from glass doors and the back of biscuit tins. Her raglan sleeves on allovers were neat and became a part of the design of the garment, quite different to the traditional set in sleeves. Her neighbour, at the time of my visit, was Elaine Buchanan.

Although not a Shetlander, Elaine had become interested in knitting and collecting patterns. She had knitted copies of two very old allovers, and in order to get the exact same shade of mustard for one dyed the

Man wearing allover.

Old allover patterns.

Old allover patterns.

51

Allover.

Landscape.

yarn with peat soot. She has trimmed baby clothes with Fair Isle and even her daughter's teddy sported a Fair Isle jumper. On square yokes she had knitted landscapes, depicting Shetland scenes and these were like a delicate water colour painting in wool. If not as skilled or adventurous as Elaine you can work out a design first using graph paper and colour pencils.

I was told of fashions over the years and the Eton collar seems to have been popular for ladies and children. One well known man, connected with the knitwear trade, said to a Yell woman that he remembered her mother — 'she was the one that did the perfect Eton Collar'. The Yell expression for squint is 'skeve as a reel', referring to the T-shaped piece of wood that wool was wound around to form hanks. Wool that was handspun was sold in hanks of 100 threads. Other notions 'don't have a sock crawin o'er Christmas' and if a person comes in 'wi' a good fit' (purposefully) when you are starting a garment means it will be quickly finished; my favourite superstition was that if you made a mistake on a jumper being knitted for a member of the family and you have to unravel it to fix the mistake then the wearer would live to wear the garment out. It was remarkable that you only worried about the family's jumpers. After all why unpick unnecessarily if knitting for profit. How different from the carpet makers of the east, who purposefully make a mistake, the Muslims believing that only the works of Allah are made truly perfect. The sums of 1s 6d as payment for a spencer was 'laid in me low', meaning placed in my hand. I liked all these quotes and superstitions and the 1x1 Fair Isle was described as mice's teeth. These details are what makes Shetland knitting personal and individual.

Not only the past was spoken of. The factories of today supply many outworkers in Yell with work. Most folk believe that what they are paid today is not on a level with other trades and many prefer to work with the private orders from south and abroad, or for small firms where the middle man does not make most of the money. I did pick up a very good machine knitting tip from Jimmy Spence of North-a-Voe. At the time he was 78 and still making away on his machine. We discussed the neck on a V-neck jumper and said how I felt that the V-necks on machine made sweaters were always poor. He said that single Vs "slag oot" and they should be knitted double. You cast on 1x1 rib on the machine and then decrease one stitch at either end until the neck is deep enough, then you increase one stitch at either end until the original number of stitches is reached. When folded in half and grafted onto the neck of the jumper there is no need to turn back any unwanted rib — 'man it's easier than trippin' in gutter'.

The women were keen to keep up with the fashions and the great standby of the Shetland household — the club book — was often consulted to find out what was in vogue. Mrs Barbara Burgess, a native of Yell, was in France demonstrating Shetland knitting and she said that the French were very keen on style rather than tradition. She was not beat and produced an outfit in grey and white which the lady displayed on a 'puppet'. The mannequin was brought and dressed in a grey knitted skirt and 2x2 rib polo neck in white, over which was worn a Fair Isle tabard in grey, white and black. Fine stockings in 2x2 rib and fashionable brogues were added to the ensemble and finally a pillbox hat and gloves completed the outfit. This combination of style and tradition caused many favourable comments from the French ladies.

Cut backs in the oil industry will no doubt affect Yell's economy. The new fashions being designed by Shetland's smaller knitwear producers may inspire some of those who, when 'needs must', return to the island to go ahead and try to earn a living with their needles in another, but not altogether different way, from their forebears.

Variations on allovers.

Allover patterns.

SHETLAND KNITTING TODAY

Many seamen and adventurers have sought the safety of Shetland's harbours and voes. During the herring boom Lerwick's streets rang with the clatter of 'Dutchie's' clogs and in the sixties the 'Norskie' fishermen were a common sight in the local bars. Soberly dressed 'Ruskies', from the Soviet factory ships, shop for sweets and luxuries in the town's shops. Oil and its related industries brought not only the Americans but a mixed bag of nationalities, some passing through, others settling in the islands and becoming part of the community. All these visitors add to the local culture and tradition.

Many of the small knitwear firms are run by 'sooth-moothers' who mix their talents with the traditional Shetland style. Some are trained in design, others have merely turned a hobby into a profitable business. One such knitter said that when she learned to knit some twenty years ago there were not many 'foreigners' around, and having learnt the basics she worked from there using crochet to join and trim many of her garments. She shaded her Fair Isle on tones of one colour to avoid 'the fruit salad look'.

Most of our greatest fashion designers are men, but those males involved in the Shetland knitwear trade tend to be more interested in finance and production than the creative side of the business.

Tommy Goudie of Gulberwick is an exception. He has been interested in fashion and new ideas for many years and is skilled in many handcrafts. Tommy has knitted jackets for himself which he then lined and wore as a smart alternative to a sports jacket; both his children were christened in gowns and shawls of his creation and many Shetland brides were married in gowns of Tommy's making. His mother was a skilled

 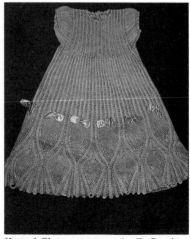

Crochet christening gown by T. Goudie.   *Knitted Christening gown by T. Goudie.*

Modern interpretation of a waistcoat.   *Modern allover in bright colours.*

knitter who decorated cardigans with freehand embroidery and overgrafted blue birds and budgies on jumpers as well as knitting variations of Fair Island openwork. In the fifties she knitted an evening top in honeycomb stitch which was then encrusted with thousands of beads and sequins. For this complex creation she received £5 and had to pay for the wool. When I visited Tommy he had recently found a five petal board wound with silk belonging to his mother, but unfortunately no silk

Overgraphted owl cardigan.

57

knitwear had survived. Another interesting point he made was that when Fair Isle jumpers were dyed black to be worn as mourning clothes all the colours took on the black dye in varying tones enabling the detailed pattern to be distinguished.

Knitters no longer produce dozens of plain crew-necks for they cannot compete with mass production from abroad, instead they design and knit more unusual garments to tempt the customer.

The Shetland Knitwear Trades Association markets knitwear on behalf of companies and individuals. Many knitters exhibit at the Autumn trade fair at Aviemore, the London shows, and attend trade and fashion fairs worldwide.

The knitwear shops on Commercial Street still sell traditional yoke jumpers and openwork scarves but many craft fairs around the islands and some interesting small shops tucked away amid Lerwick's lanes offer a wider choice of knitwear to cater for more individual tastes.

Louise Joffre's stylish fisher-ribs and Victoria Gibson's textured mixed yarn sweaters and coats are moving away from traditional styles while Stakkatak's colour themed tiny patterned allovers and Anne Gibson's sweaters patterned with shells and landscapes interpret the tradition in a modern way.

The Shetland Workshop Gallery sells Hazel Simpson's allovers. In my opinion these are among the best of today's designs. Her machined range include modern shapes in subtle blends reminiscent of the soft Shetland tweeds.

Although the Fair Isle yoked dresses of the sixties were popular no-one seems to have produced a successful dress since. In the south the small knitwear firms sell leggings and tube skirts to team up with more exotic jumpers. This idea may be worth copying.

The agricultural shows at Walls, Voe and Cunningsburgh could perhaps include a high fashion class in the knitwear section. As a child I can recall Theodora Coutts' knitwear shop displaying prize-winning knitwear from the shows, the winning ticket in a prominent place.

Mohair and cotton are used more frequently now, both on their own and mixed with Shetland wools. Hunter's of Brora are always updating their colour ranges and have recently brought out a thick yarn called Unst Fleece which is good for textured knitting. The spinning mill run by Jamieson's at Sandness, on the west side of Shetland, produces 100% pure Shetland wool and the colour range is increasing.

The selection of knitting books on sale in the local bookshop offers much source material to inspire knitters. Cross stitch embroidery books are another useful source of patterns especially suitable for overgrafting. These designs can be used for knitting, but often the number of threads to be carried makes for complications.

Ideas come from many sources and as I travelled the islands researching this book I became more and more impressed by the inventiveness of the Shetland women. Inspiration could be a biscuit box or a spectacular sunset.

I no longer live in Shetland, but I would like to thank all the knitters who gave me their help in compiling this book. I think of them often and hope they approve the end result and it is to them that I dedicate this work. The firms may come and go, fashions and trends will change but without the skills and patience of these hardworking women there would not be a Shetland knitwear industry. Pins and graph books will no doubt be replaced by machine and computer tapes but through all progress the human hand must be the guide.

Spinning by hand with spindle.

Spinning using spinning wheel.

Lace Patterns

Cat's Paw

1st row: K7 * wf, K2tog, K6 * repeat from * to end
2nd row: Knit
3rd row: K5 * K2tog, wf, K1, wf, K2tog, K3 * repeat from * to last 10 sts, K2tog, wf, K1, wf, K2tog, K5
4th row: Knit
5th row: K4 * K2tog, wf, K3, wf, K2tog, K1 * repeat from * to last 11 sts, K2tog, wf, K3, wf, K2tog, K4
6th row: Knit
7th row: K6 * wf, K3tog, wf, K5 * repeat from * to last 9 sts, wf, K3tog, wf, K6
8th row: Knit
9th row: Knit
10th row: Knit
11th row: K11 * wf, K2tog, K6 * repeat from * to last 4 sts, K4
12th row: Knit
13th row: K9 * K2tog, wf, K1, wf, K2tog, K3 * repeat from * to last 6 sts, K6
14th row: Knit
15th row: K8 * K2tog, wf, K3, wf, K2tog, K1 * repeat from * to last 7 sts, K7
16th row: Knit
17th row: K10 * wf, K3tog, wf, K5 * repeat from * to last 5 sts, K5
18th row: Knit
19th row: Knit
20th row: Knit

Bird's Eye

1st row: K4 * wf, K3tog, wf, K3 repeat from * to last 7 sts, wf, K3tog, wf, K4
2nd row: K2, K2tog * wf, K3, wf, K3tog * repeat to last 7 sts, wf, K3, wf, K2tog, K2
3rd row: K3 * wf, K2tog, K1, K2tog, wf, K1 * repeat to last 2 sts, K2
4th row: K3 * wf, K2tog, wf, K3tog, wf, K1 * repeat to last 8 sts, wf, K2tog, wf, K3tog, wf, K3
5th row: Repeat row 3
6th row: Repeat row 1
7th row: K3 * K2tog, wf, K1, wf, K2tog, K1 * repeat to last 3 sts, K3
8th row: K3, K2tog, wf, K1, wf, K2tog * wf, K3tog, wf, K1, wf, K2tog * repeat from * to last 3 sts, K3
9th row: Repeat row 7
10th row: Repeat row 2

To continue repeat from row 3 to 10 only as often as required

Fern Stitch

1st row: *K1, wf, K2tog, K5, K2tog, wf* repeat to last st, K1
2nd row: Purl
3rd row: *K1, wf, K1, K2tog, K3, K2tog, K1, wf* repeat to last st, K1
4th row: Purl
5th row: *K1, wf, K2, K2tog, K1, K2tog, K2, wf* repeat to last st, K1
6th row: Purl
7th row: *K1, wf, K3, K3tog, K3, wf* repeat to last st, K1
8th row: Purl
9th row: *K3, K2tog, wf, K1, wf, K2tog, K2* repeat to last st, K1
10th row: Purl
11th row: *K2, K2tog, K1, wf, K1, wf, K1, K2tog, K1* to last st, K1
12th row: Purl
13th row: *K1, K2tog, K2, wf, K1, wf, K2, K2tog* to last st, K1
14th row: Purl
15th row: K2tog*K3, wf, K1, wf, K3, K3tog* repeat from * to last 2 sts, K2
16th row: Purl

Small Diamond

1st row: K2*K2tog, wf, K1, wf, K2tog, K1* repeat from * to last st, K1
2nd row: Knit
3rd row: K1, K2tog*wf, K3, wf, K3tog* repeat from * to last 6 sts, wf, K3, wf, K2tog, K1
4th row: Knit
5th row: K2*wf, K2tog, K1, K2tog, wf, K1* repeat from * to last st, K1
6th row: Knit
7th row: K3*wf, K3tog, wf, K3* repeat from * to end
8th row: Knit

Hap Shell

1st row: (K2tog) 3 times, (wf, K1) 6 times, (K2tog) 3 times, repeat to end
2nd row: Knit
3rd row: Knit
4th row: Knit
5th row: Knit
6th row: Knit

Print and Wave

1st row: *K4, wf, K2tog, wf, K2tog, wf, K2, K2tog, K2tog, K2, wf, K1, repeat from * to end

2nd row: Purl

3rd row: K2, K2tog*wf, K2tog, wf, K2tog, wf, K1, wf, K2, K2tog, K4, K2tog, K2, repeat from * to last 13 sts, wf, K2tog, wf, K2tog, wf, K2tog, wf, K1, wf, K2, K2tog, K4

4th row: Purl

5th row: K1, K2tog*wf, K2tog, wf, K2tog, wf, K3, wf, K2, K2tog, K2, K2tog, K2, repeat from * to last 14 sts, wf, K2tog, wf, K2tog, wf, K3, wf, K2, K2tog, K3

6th row: Purl

7th row: K2tog*wf, K2tog, wf, K2tog, wf, K5, wf, K2, K2tog, K2tog, K2, repeat from * to last 15 sts, wf, K2tog, wf, K2tog, wf, K5, wf, K2, K2tog, K2

8th row: Purl

9th row: K2*wf, K2tog, wf, K2tog, wf, K2, K2tog, K4, K2tog, K2, wf, K1, repeat from * to last 15 sts, wf, K2tog, wf, K2tog, wf, K2, K2tog, K7

10th row: Purl

11th row: *K3, wf, K2tog, wf, K2tog, wf, K2, K2tog, K2, K2tog, K2, wf, repeat from * to last 17 sts, K3, wf, K2tog, wf, K2tog, wf, K2, K2tog, K6

12th row: Purl

Pattern Section

Fair Isle base jumper
(Introduction, photograph page 3)

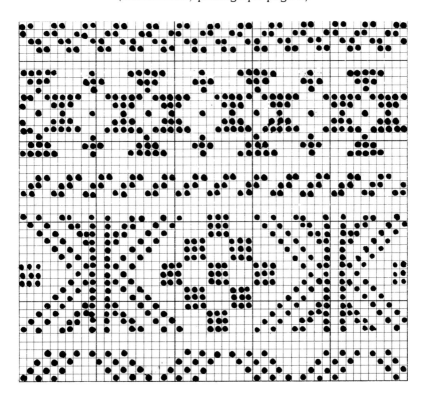

Child's scarf

(Fair Isle, photograph page 13)

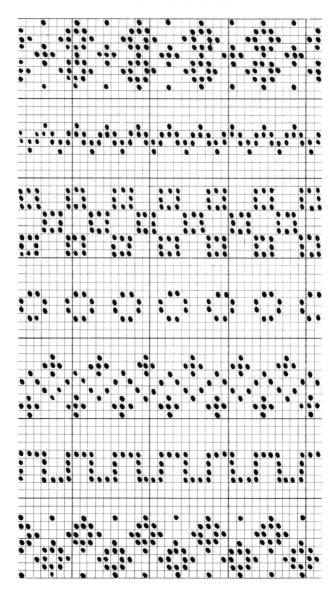

(continued on facing page)

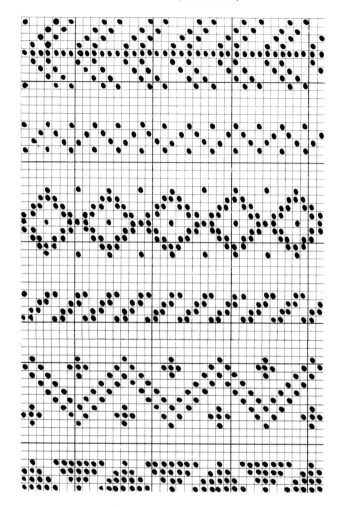

(continued overleaf)

Child's scarf *(continued)*

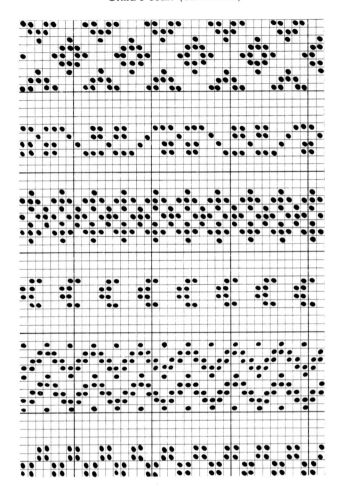

Fair Isle Allover

(Fair Isle, photograph page 20)

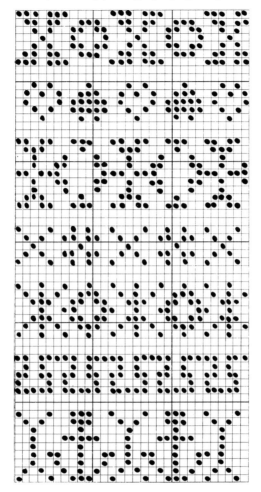

(continued overleaf)

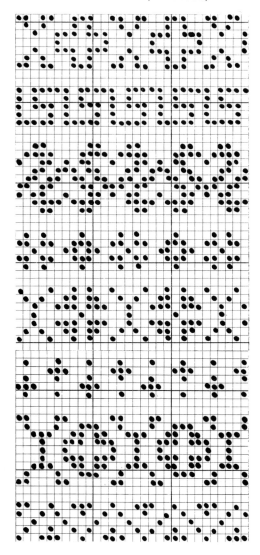

70

Fair Isle Allover

(Fair Isle, photograph page 15)

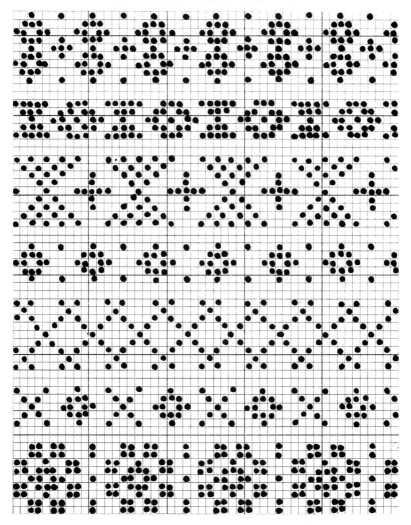

(continued overleaf)

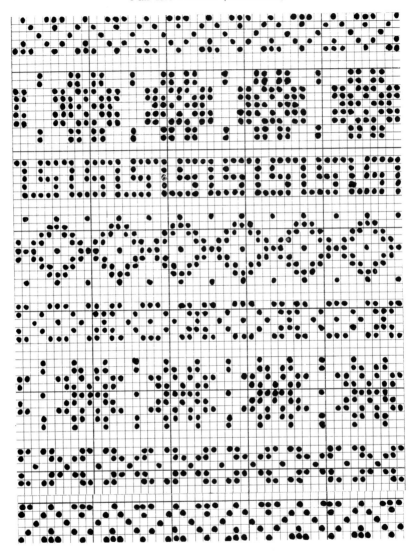

72

Norwegian Lumber

(Skerries, photograph page 38)

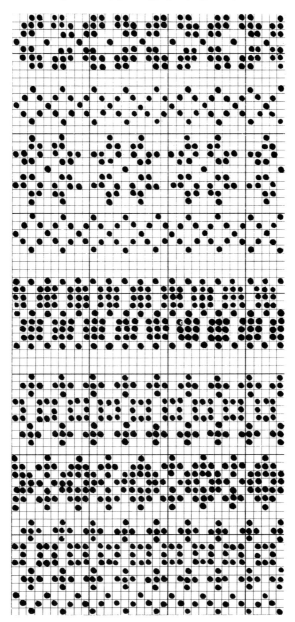

(continued overleaf)

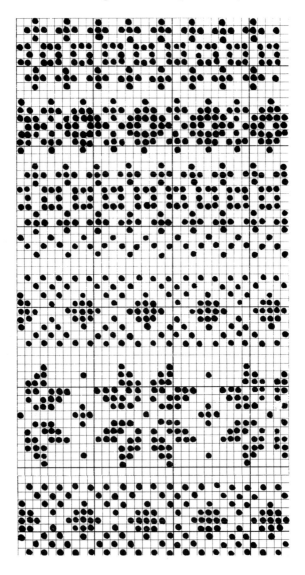

Fisherman's Jumper

(Skerries, photograph page 37)

(continued overleaf)

75

Fisherman's Jumper *(continued)*

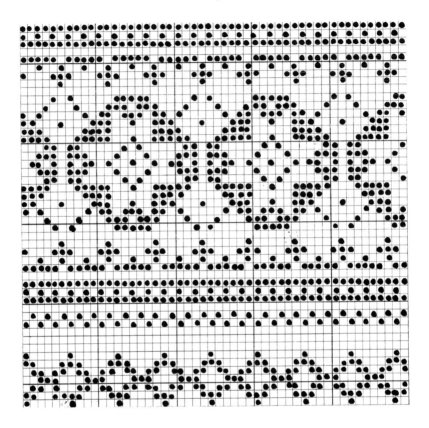

Suggestions for Fair Isle Allover

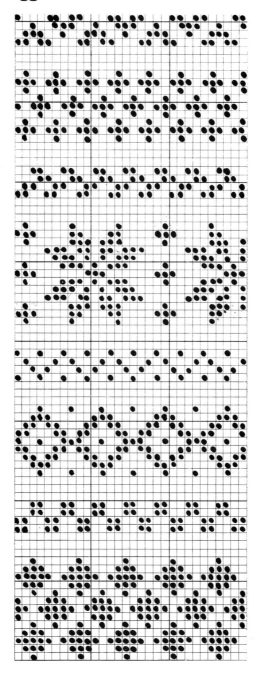

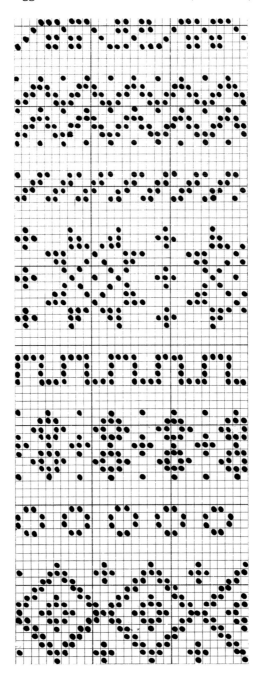

78

Churchill pattern
(Unst, page 28)

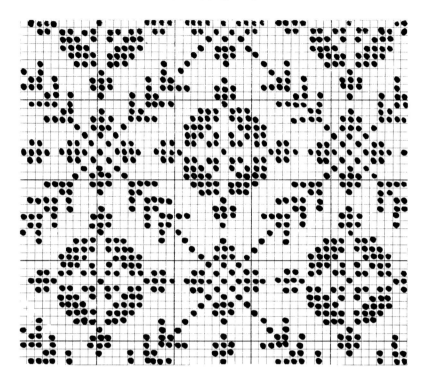

A. Pagoda pattern
B. Intaking Anchor
(Unst, page 26)

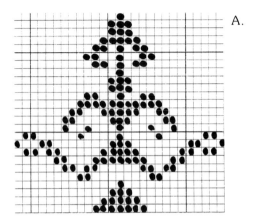

A.

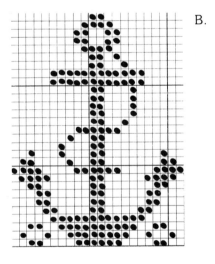

B.

Selection of Star Patterns

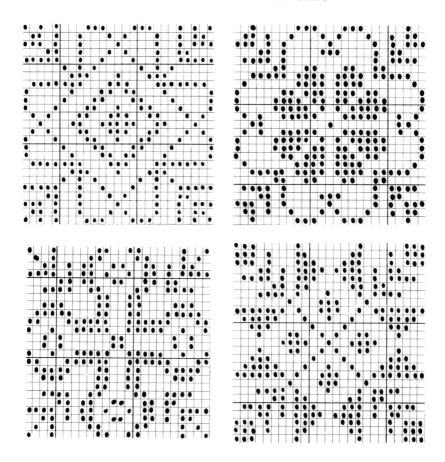

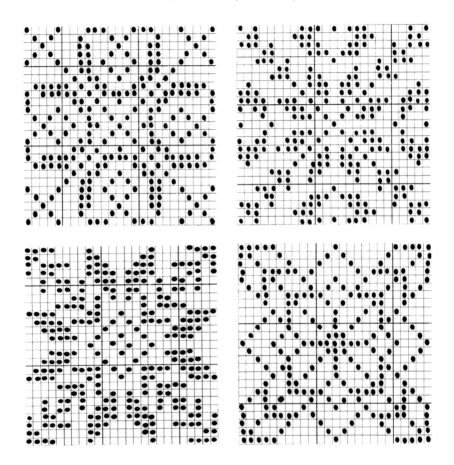

82

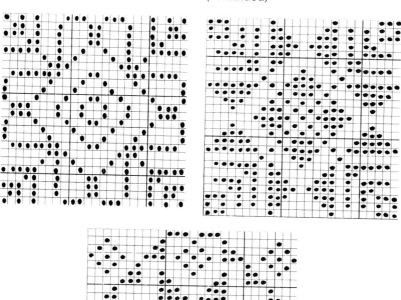

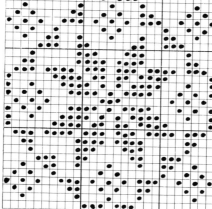

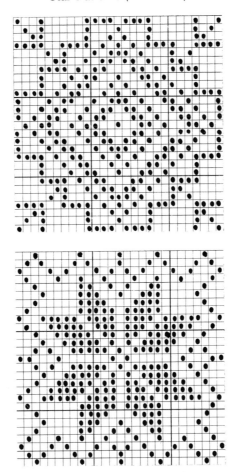

84

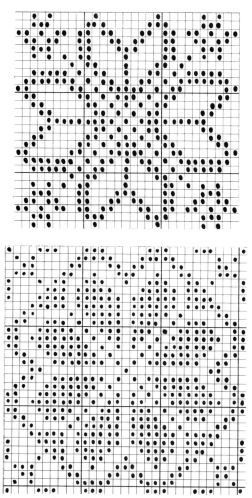

85

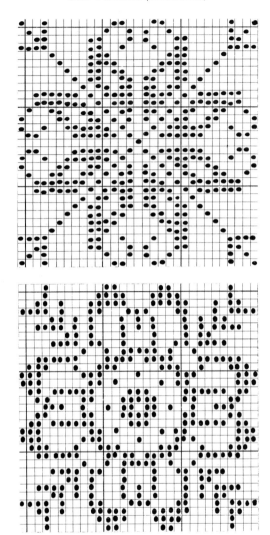

86

Various Component Patterns
and Allover Designs

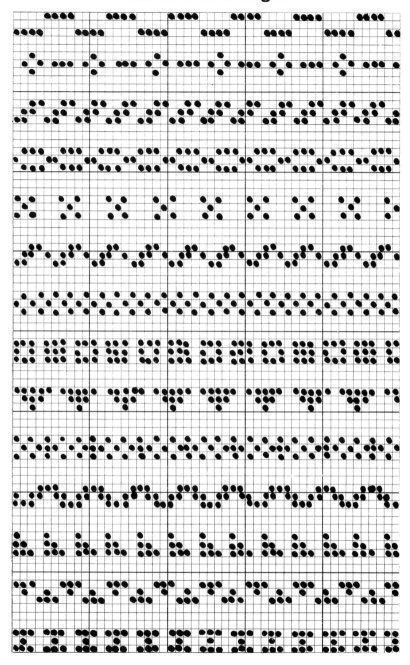

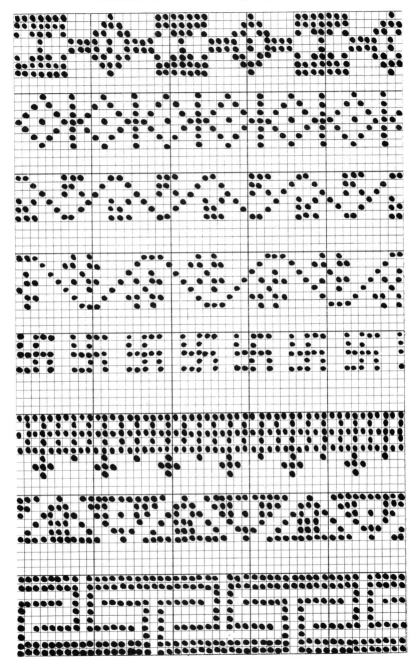

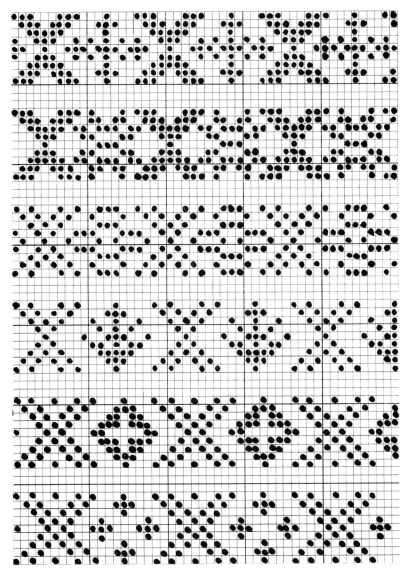

89

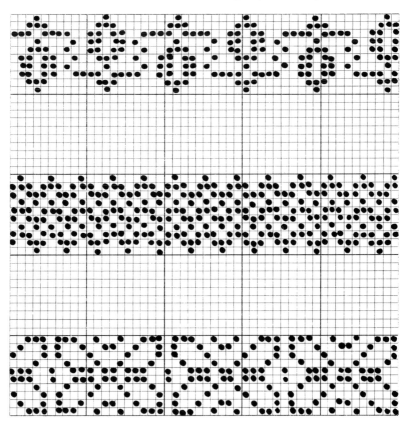

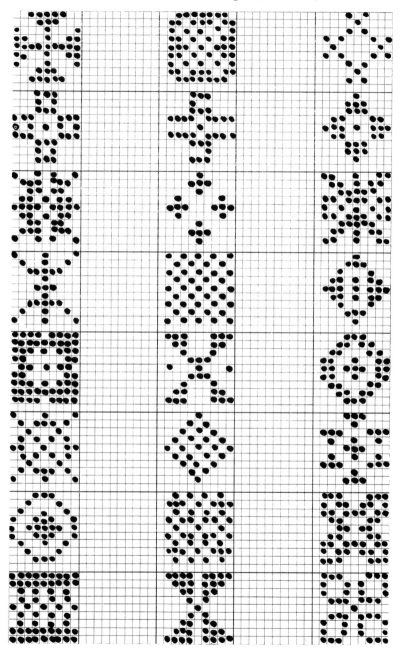

91

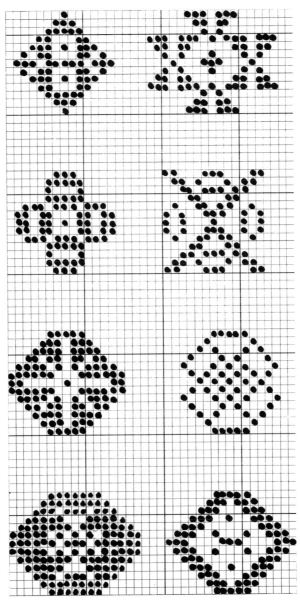

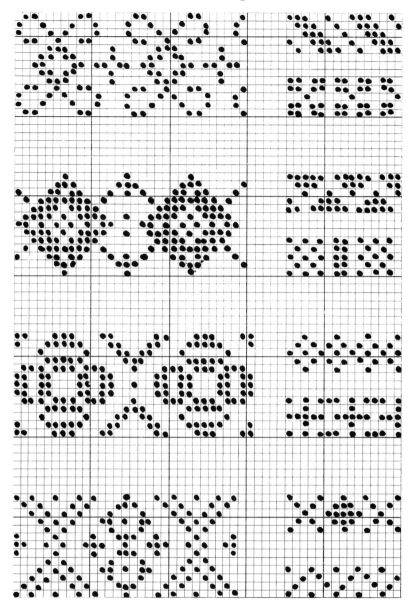

93

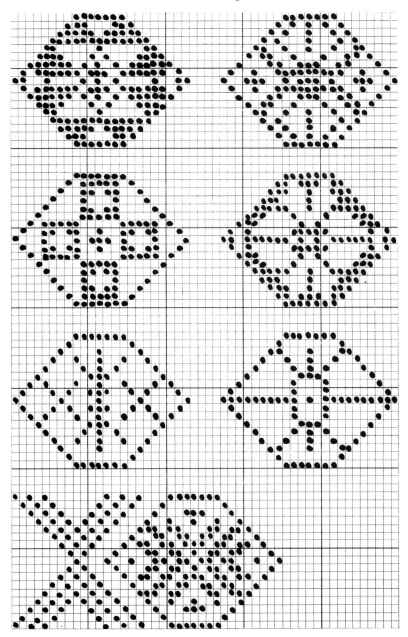

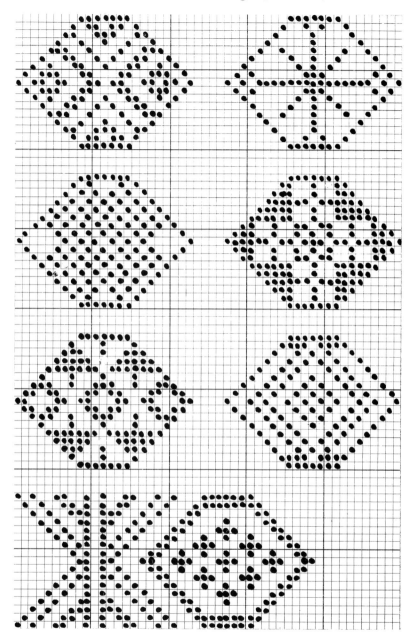

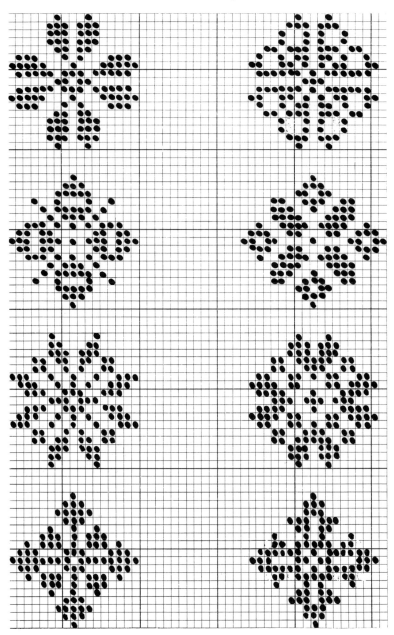

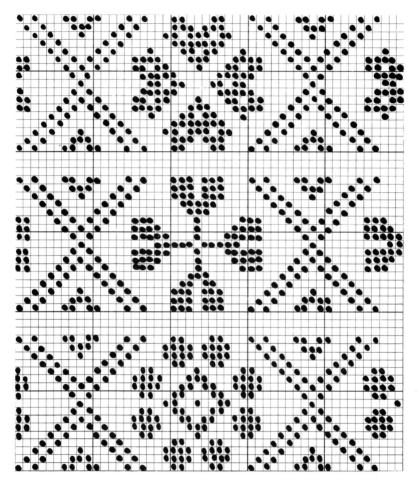

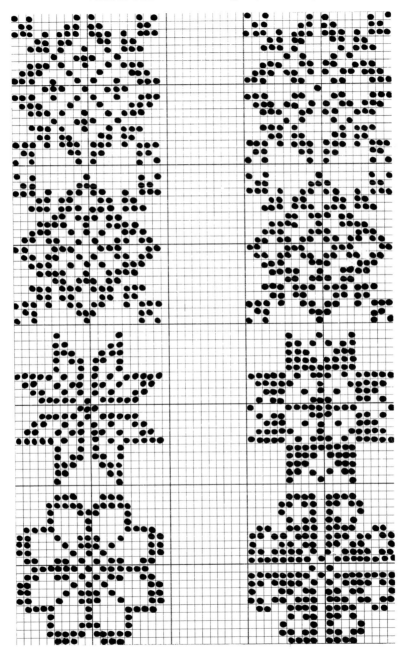

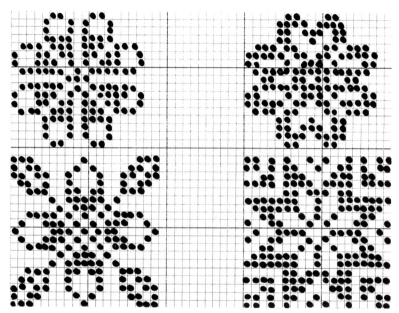

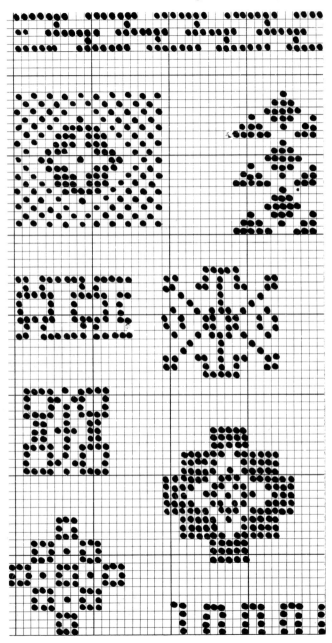

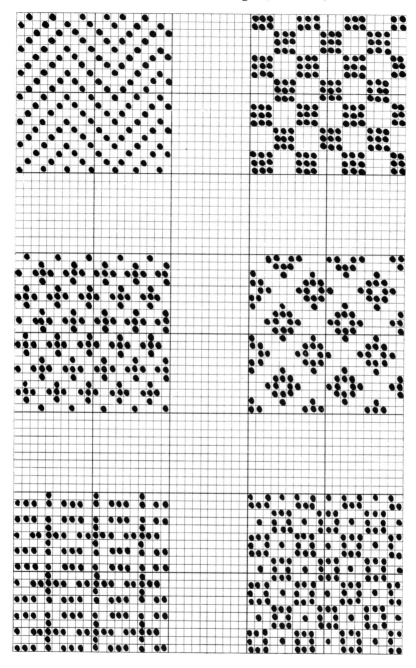

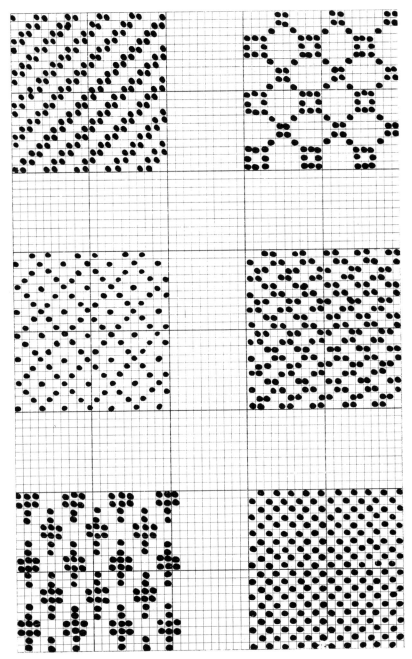

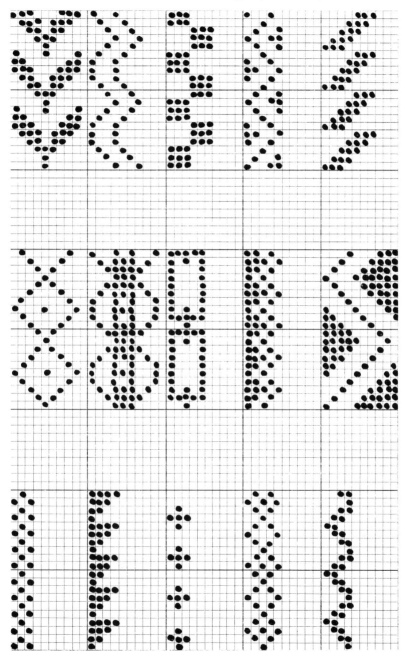

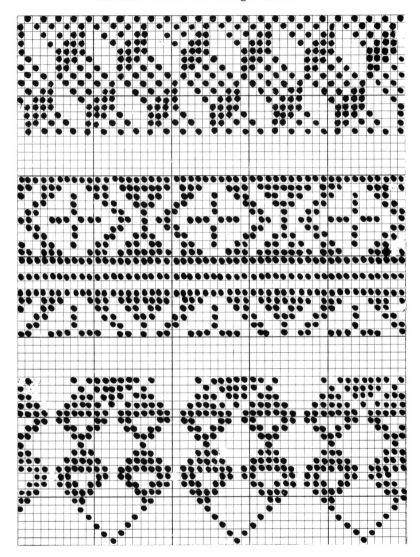

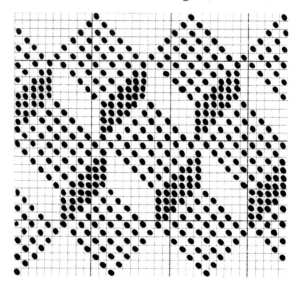

Various Patterns and Designs *(continued)*

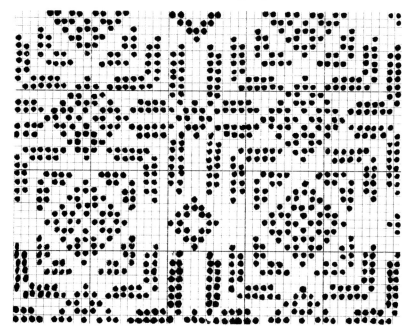

Various Patterns and Designs *(continued)*

110

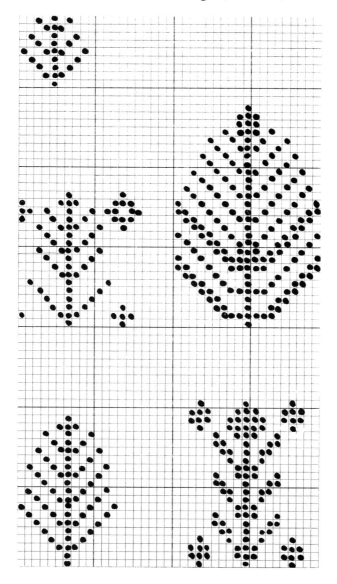

Old Patterns
From Robbie Williamson's pattern book (Unst, page 29)

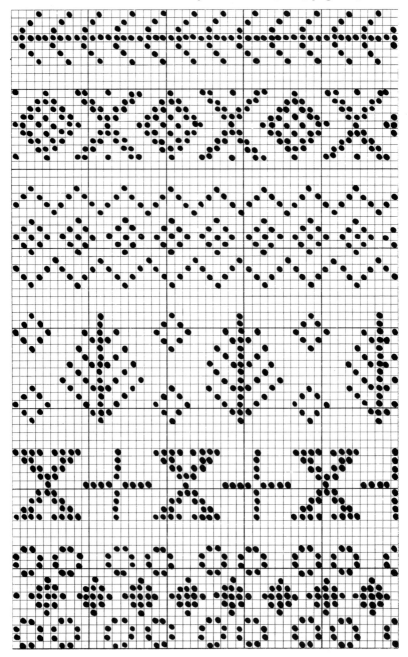

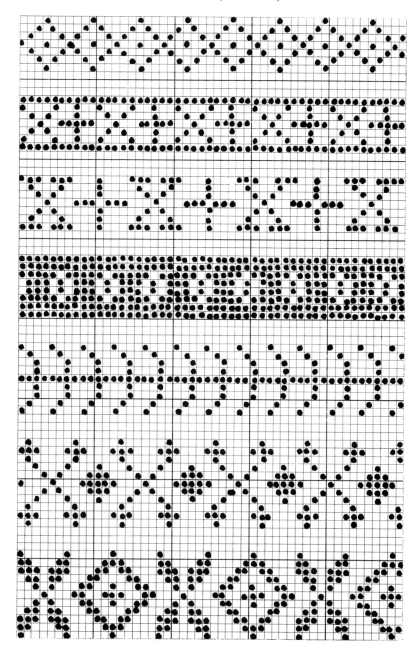

113

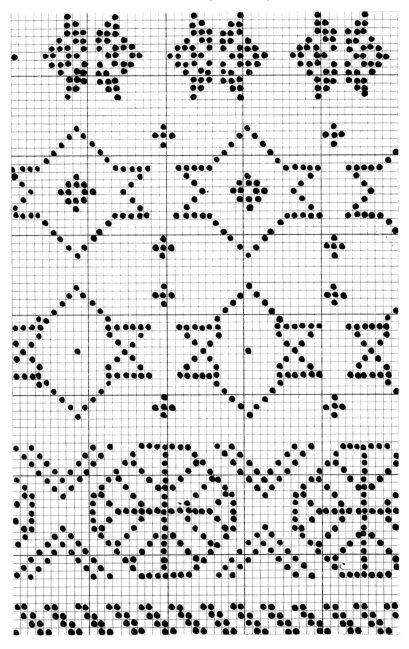

114

115

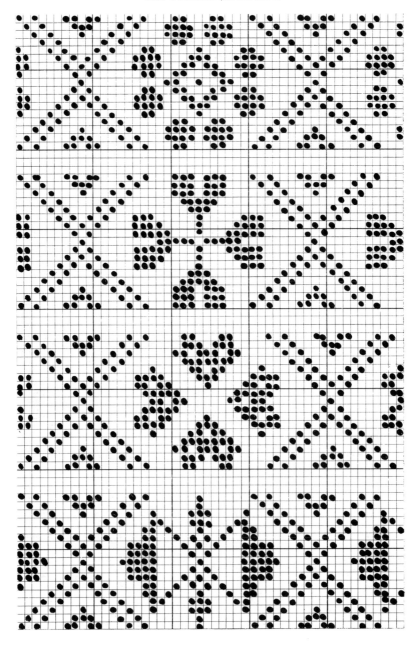

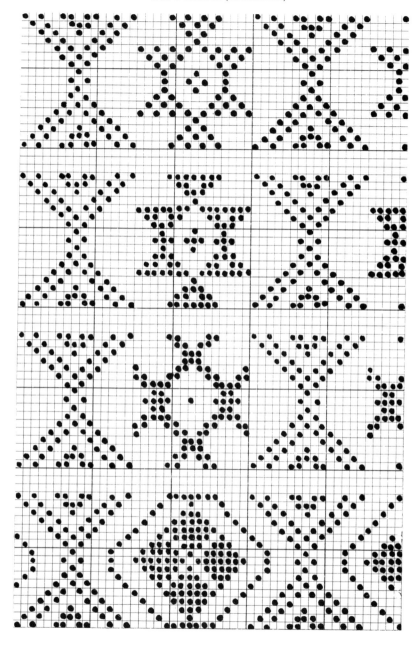

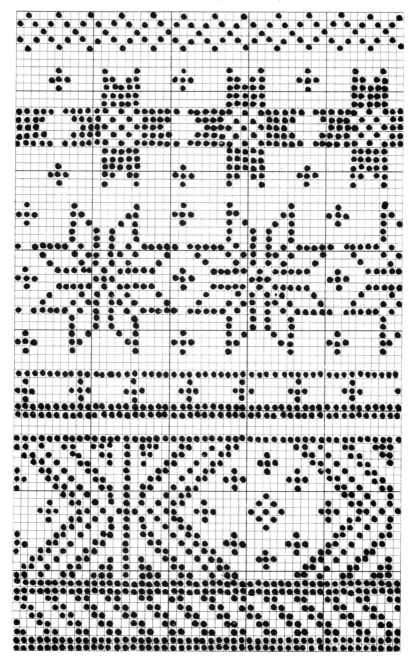

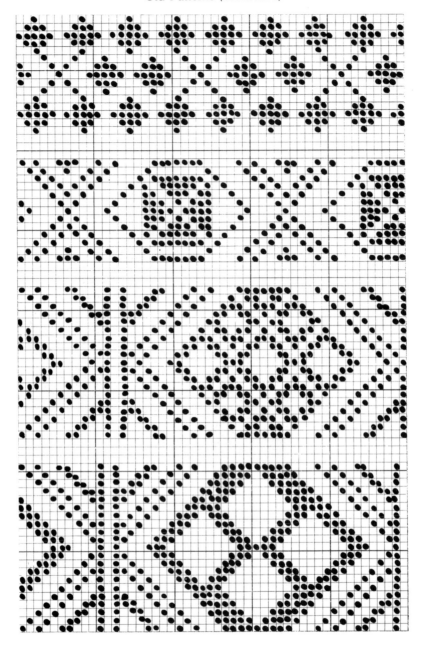

HUSFLIDEN

Markensgaten 24 - Telefon 2606

KRISTIANSAND S.

TORRIDALSTRØYA

ST. 50. ST. 42 OG 6 ÅR

Trøya er laget etter tre gamle modeller som vi har funnet i Torridalen ved Kristiansand S. Mønsterbordene var litt forskjellig plasert på disse. Fargene kan varieres etter ønske. Mest ble brukt blått/rødt. men også rødt/hvitt og blått/hvitt kan brukes.

Glossary

Allover	allover patterned garment
Basque	rib or waist
Cloo bag	bag containing odd scraps of wool often used up in Fair Isle knitting
Colly lamp	small open iron lamp with wick floating in fish oil
Cot	long skirt often striped
Cradle strap	strip of knitting or fabric laced over infant in cradle
Craigs	rocks at foreshore
Creepie	small three-legged stool
Dell	dig
Dress	wash and stretch over a shaped board — glove, jumper, scarf board, etc.
E'ed	eyelid
Flo'ers	larger Fair Isle motifs
Gansey	jumper
Grunds	name of border patterns on Fair Isle
Haaf	deep sea beyond coastal waters. Deep sea fishing carried out 30-40 miles offshore in open boats
Haaf cap	conical shaped knitted hat
Hap	hand-knitted shawl
Half a crown	a silver coin worth 2s 6d or 12½ new pence
Helly	weekend
Kishie	straw basket or creel
Knitting belt	belt of sealskin or leather with a horsehair stuffed pad punched with holes that support knitting needles
Knitting sheath	similar to knitting belt but with feathers bound together to form needle support
Loops	stitches
Lumber jacket	knitted garment with front buttoning to neck
Makkin	knitting
Muffler	long scarf
Peerie	small
Rivlins	shoe made from untanned animal hide, hair outermost
Roo	to pluck wool off a sheep
Semmit	man's vest
Sock	knitting
Spencer	lightweight knitted vest
Wife	woman
Wire	knitting needle
Yule	Christmas

NOTES

NOTES

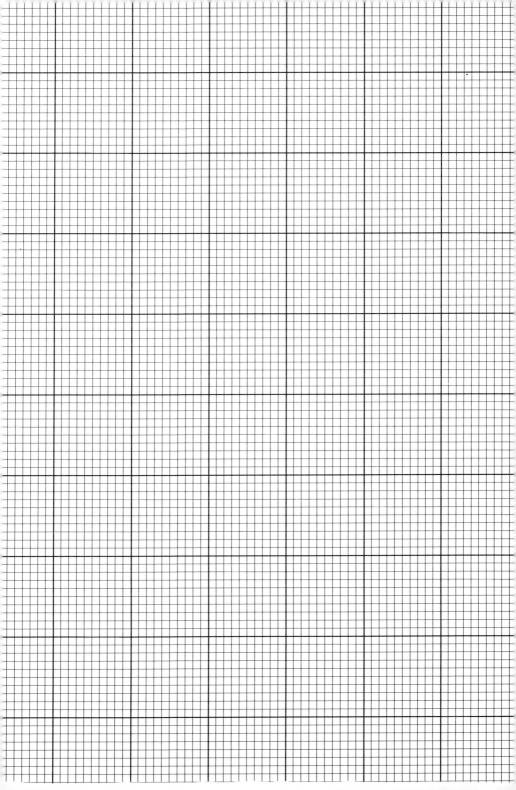

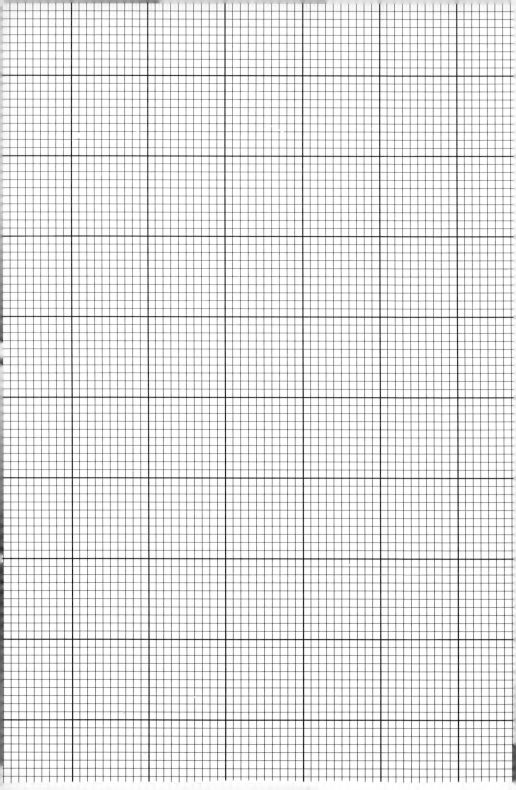

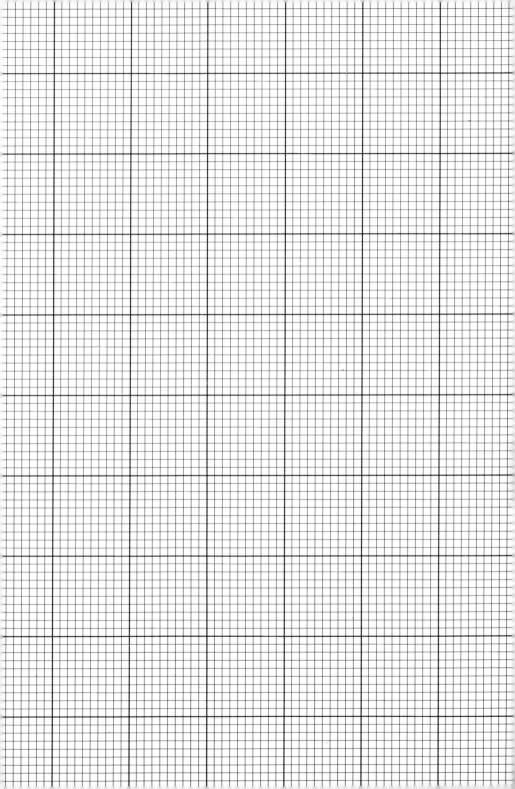

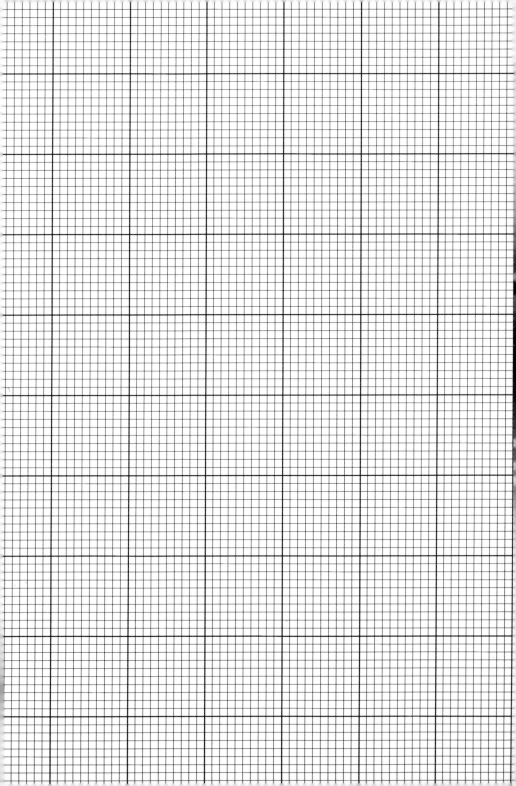